C000216553

To Eawin

# OUR GOD HEALS

with love + blessings

Fr. Nicholas

First published in 2016 by
New Life Publishing, Luton
Bedfordshire LU4 9HG

Copyright © 2016 Nicholas Broadbridge OSB

Editor: George Jerjian
Assistant editors:
Liz Martinez and Marie-Colette Gradwell

British Library Cataloguing in Publication Data
A catalogue record for this book is available
from the British Library

**ISBN 978 1 903623 97 8**

Front cover:
Jesus Heals the Paralytic by Harold Copping (1907)
*Courtesy: http://truthbook.com/jesus-paintings/*
*jesus-heals-the-paralytic-by-harold-copping*

Typesetting by Goodnews Books, Luton, UK
www.goodnewsbooks.net   01582 571011
Printed and bound in Great Britain

# OUR GOD HEALS

## To Set Free Those Who Are Oppressed

Fr. Nicholas Broadbridge OSB

# CONTENTS

# FOREWORD

I have known Fr. Nicholas Broadbridge since the early 1980s, mainly through the Catholic Charismatic Renewal, and have always greatly appreciated the talks he has given and our discussions about the Holy Spirit and the ministries of healing and deliverance. My own position as President of the Council of International Catholic Charismatic Renewal Services (ICCRS) for over 10 years, my ecumenical work, particularly with the International Charismatic Consultation and as co-chair of the Charismatic and Pentecostal Leaders Annual Conference, and my membership of the National Service Committee for the Catholic Charismatic Renewal in England, have all brought me into frequent contact with people from all over the world who are directly involved in the healing ministry. I can honestly say that I have found the Healing Workshops of Fr. Nicholas, as explained in *'Our God Heals'*, as helpful as anything else I have come across since my Baptism in the Holy Spirit in 1976.

Why do I say this? Because in this remarkable book, Fr. Nicholas draws on many years of careful thought and study, all brought to reality through his practical experience of giving the resultant teaching workshops which are admirably illustrated by the stories, testimonies and examples contained in page after page of his book. His is not just a theological and interesting approach, but the presentation of his lived experience of ministering in the complex areas of healing and deliverance, all backed up with remarkable stories of changed lives and supported by the wisdom of other well respected writers.

His Healing Workshops are helpfully divided into three clear sections. Firstly - *Love Forgiveness Healing*; followed by *The Ministry of Deliverance*; and thirdly *The Gift and the Gifts of the Spirit.* Each section contains refreshing definitions and insights, supported by challenging questions, which cause the reader to pause for thought. I really liked the clear association between love and forgiveness in section 1, reminding us that lack of forgiveness stops love flowing, and the definition of Inner Healing as *'simply God's love flowing through us'*.

This is maintenance to mission. I am deliberately quoting several simple statements, but please believe that Fr. Nicholas's unpacking and development of these is both creative and thought-provoking, containing great wisdom and practical experience.

I could write much more about this fascinating book, but the purpose of my foreword is to give the reader just a flavor of the writer's approach and the content, hoping that this will be enough to stimulate a desire to read and reflect on the wisdom and teaching that follow.

Fr. Nicholas Broadbridge has performed a great public service by making his years of experience of his Healing Workshops available to us all *to set free those who are oppressed* and I am firmly convinced we owe him a deep debt of gratitude which we can best repay by carefully reading and reflecting on *Our God Heals*.

*Charles Whitehead KSG*
*13 August 2015*

# HEALING WORKSHOP

# I

# LOVE

# FORGIVENESS

# HEALING

I T HAPPENED THE DAY MY MOTHER DIED on January 2nd 1974. Normally, all the monks stay at Douai Abbey for Christmas Day and occasionally some go away for a few days at New Year. I went home that year and I was home on January 2nd. My mother, who was neither an invalid nor even a semi-invalid, had been in bed a few days with bronchitis. The doctor had been to see her that morning and given her some new medicine.

That evening at about 10:00, my niece called my sister to go upstairs because my mother was not responding when spoken to and was lying with her eyes closed. My niece thought she was asleep but when my sister looked closer she found that my mother was dead.

I was downstairs in the kitchen, playing cards with my two nephews. The question in my mind was: 'Why was I not at my mother's bedside when she was dying?' After all I was a priest. 'Shouldn't I have been with her during her last few moments on earth?' I think I realised deep down inside me that I felt guilty not being with her in her last moments and that I needed something to take away that feeling of guilt. People would tell me that I had done nothing wrong but that did not lessen my feeling of guilt.

I didn't know what that something was.
Nowadays we would call it **healing**.

## THE DIFFERENCE BETWEEN HEALING AND CURING

Many people do not realise that there is a tremendous difference between Healing and Curing, so I give two analogies to show the difference.

The first analogy to show the difference between healing and curing is the difference between a hospital and a hospice. In a hospital they are trying to *cure* whereas in a hospice they are not. The hospital is concerned with the *body* whilst the hospice is concerned with the *spirit*, that is with the *whole person*, to allow the person to have peace whilst still living and peace as they are *dying*. This is a form of healing.

The second analogy can be shown in the parable of the ten lepers:

Luke 17: 12   *'...He was met by ten lepers, who stood at a distance and lifted up their voices and said, 'Jesus, Master, have mercy on us.' When he saw them he said to them, 'Go and show yourselves to the priests.' And as they went they were cleansed... Then one of them, when he saw that he was **healed**, turned back, praising God with a loud voice; and he fell on his face at Jesus' feet, giving him thanks. Now he was a Samaritan. Then said Jesus, 'Were not ten cleansed? Where are the nine? Rise and go your way; your faith has made you whole.'*

This shows us that **ten** have been **cured** and **one** has been **healed**.

***Healing of Ten Lepers by James Tissot, (c.1890)***
*Courtesy: The Brooklyn Museum, New York*

## HEALING MINISTRY

I think it is fair to say that people don't go into the Healing Ministry because they want to, but rather because they are pushed into it by God. What started me off was someone selling me the book *Healing* by Francis MacNutt. It is very good and gives the general background of Healing. As I read it, I was fascinated because it was telling me, who had been ordained 14 years and had studied Philosophy and Theology, something that I had never been told before. It was so simple - the Gospels were full of Christ's stories of miracles and healings. Was it a coincidence or one of those God instances that I came across Charismatic Renewal at the same time in 1975? As far as I can tell, most people in the Healing Ministry arrive by the same route.

It was shortly after this that I began to be invited to give talks at Charismatic Conferences and at Days of Renewal, when Prayer Groups come together once a month, but I was not yet into the Ministry of Healing. I was drawn in gradually by joining in with groups who were praying **with** (not **for**, but **with**) people who had asked for healing prayer. This is of paramount importance in explaining Praying for Healing. Praying **with** and praying **for** are two completely different things. The ministry of praying **with** people is very common at the end of each session of a Charismatic Prayer Group meeting. You pray there and then **with** the person, not later when you get home and say your prayers, and almost always with **the laying on of hands** which is an ancient gesture as in:

Acts 8: 17 *'Then they laid [their] hands on them, and they received the Holy Spirit,'* and in

2 Timothy 1: 6 *'Hence I remind you to rekindle the gift of God (Holy Spirit) that is within you through the laying on of my hands;'*

Later, when I had finished teaching at Douai School, I was asked to take over the nearby parishes of Pangbourne and Theale and I almost immediately began to conduct a Healing Service once a month at Pangbourne Parish. This continued from 1985 until 1990 when I was asked to take over the parish of Malvern in Worcestershire. Again, I took a Healing Service once a month and this continued until 1993 when all the local churches suggested that this Healing Service might be shared among them and the relevant minister in each church would take the service himself. It went on like this until I was moved to another of the Douai parishes at Alcester in 1994, where once more I took a Healing Service once a month.

In fact I was still at Malvern Parish when it was arranged that I would come back to conduct a Healing Workshop once a year at Douai Abbey. Then I had a serious car accident in Alcester in 1995, which saw me back at Douai for eight months learning to walk again. I returned to Alcester for just eight months until I was recalled to Douai permanently. Back home at Douai, I began to conduct workshops more frequently. Many of the people who came to my Healing Workshop 1, as it was called, wanted to continue and begged for more. That was how Healing Workshop 2 started. Again people wanted more and I had to start Healing Workshop 3 and even then I had participants who had done all three workshops who wanted more and I arranged for them to come as a group twice a year for three or four years. That had to stop because I was told I was booking too many Saturdays. Some of them have come back and done the workshops again.

I always started my workshops and each of the four sessions in the day with the following prayers:

*Come Holy Spirit, fill the hearts of your faithful*
*and enkindle in them the fire of your love.*
*Send forth your Spirit and they shall be created*
*and you shall renew the face of the earth.*

*O God, who has taught the hearts of the faithful*
*by the light of the Holy Spirit, grant that by the gift*
*of the same Spirit, we may be always truly wise*
*and ever rejoice in his consolation*
*through Christ Our Lord.   Amen*

*ooo0ooo*

*Oh, Holy Spirit, beloved of my soul. I adore you.*
*Enlighten me, guide me, strengthen me, console me.*
*Tell me what I should do... give me your orders.*
*I promise to submit myself to all that you desire of me*
*and to accept all that you permit to happen to me.*
*Let me only know your will.*

## THE HOLY SPIRIT IN THE LIFE OF JESUS

The Catechism of the Catholic Church teaches us about the Holy Trinity:

> [255] The divine persons are relative to one another. Because it does not divide the divine unity, the real distinction of the persons from one another resides solely in the relationships which relate them to one another: 'In the relational names of the persons the Father is related to the Son, the Son to the Father, and the Holy Spirit to both. While they are called three persons in view of their relations, we believe in one nature or substance'. Indeed 'everything (in them) is one where there is no opposition of relationship'. 'Because of that unity the Father is wholly in the Son and wholly in the Holy Spirit; the Son is wholly in the Father and wholly in the Holy Spirit; the Holy Spirit is wholly in the Father and wholly in the Son.'[1]

The same Catechism states in the Profession of Faith that there is a Joint Mission of the Son and the Spirit:

[689] The One whom the Father has sent into our hearts, the Spirit of his Son, is truly God. Consubstantial with the Father and the Son, the Spirit is inseparable from them, in both the inner life of the Trinity and his gift of love for the world. In adoring the Holy Trinity, life-giving, consubstantial, and indivisible, the Church's faith also professes the distinction of persons. When the Father sends his Word, he always sends his Breath. In their joint mission, the Son and the Holy Spirit are distinct but inseparable. To be sure, it is Christ who is seen, the visible image of the invisible God, but it is the Spirit who reveals him.

[690] Jesus is Christ, 'anointed', because the Spirit is his anointing, and everything that occurs from the Incarnation on, derives from this fullness. When Christ is finally glorified, he can in turn send the Spirit from his place with the Father to those who believe in him: he communicates to them his glory, that is, the Holy Spirit who glorifies him. From that time

on, this joint mission will be manifested in the children adopted by the Father in the Body of his Son: the mission of the Spirit of adoption is to unite them to Christ and make them live in him...'[2]

As it states in [689] above, the Spirit is God's *'gift of love for the world.'* I used to start my workshops with the Cross, explaining that Jesus Christ loved us so much that he died for us as our Redeemer, because 'love' is the most important word in healing. I once heard a story about a little girl who asked Jesus in prayer how much he loved us; he stretched out his arms and said to her, 'this much.'

In 1998, the *Year of the Spirit* for us Catholics, I was asked to give the three talks on the Holy Spirit in the middle of the Alpha Course to the parish of St Edmund Campion in Maidenhead. Since that time, up till recently, I have given those same three talks 30 times. As you may gather, I began to find out much more about the Holy Spirit, so much so that I was once accused of being obsessed with the 'Holy

Spirit'. At the same time, I was reading Fr. Raniero Cantalamessa's book *The Holy Spirit in the Life of Jesus* where he writes:

*'It is vitally important therefore to find out from the Gospels just what the Holy Spirit prompted Jesus to do during his life on earth, what steps he made him take, what choices: for he is prompting the church to do exactly the same thing now.'* [3]

Moreover, Jesus also says to his disciples and to us as well:

John 14: 12 *'Truly, truly, I say to you, he who believes in me will also do the works that I do; and greater works than these will he do, because I go to the Father.'*

Cantalamessa explains, *'that Jesus' whole life unfolded under the action of the Holy Spirit; within this continual presence however, certain particular moments stand out, since the Gospels themselves explicitly relate them to a special prompting of Jesus by the Holy Spirit.*

*There are three such moments in particular: the Spirit drives Jesus out into the wilderness to be tempted (Mark*

*1: 22); the Spirit consecrates Jesus by anointing him to bring the glad tidings to the poor (Luke 4: 18); the Spirit makes Jesus 'exult' and say, (page 22)'I bless you Father...' (Luke10: 21). In other words the Spirit urges Jesus on, to struggle against the devil, to preach the gospel, and to pray to the Father and offer himself in sacrifice to him.*[4]

In the struggle with the devil, *'Jesus fulfils his kingly mission in that he overthrows the kingdom of Satan and establishes the kingdom of God; he himself said, 'If it is by the Spirit of God that I drive out demons then the kingdom of God has come upon you (Matt 12: 28); ...Thus in all these three things (in the above paragraph) he performs his fundamental mission as Servant of Yahweh, which he received at his baptism and in which all other activities are included.'*[5]

These activities include expulsion of demons (as in Mark 1:23 onwards) where a man with an unclean spirit cries out *'what have you to do with us, Jesus of Nazareth?' But Jesus rebuked him saying, 'Be silent and come out of him...'* On this point, Cantalamessa writes, *'Most striking is the authority and power bursting forth from Jesus. Immediately people begin to ask: Where does this authority come from? The answer from the hostile is: From the prince of demons! Jesus's answer is: From the Holy Spirit. 'By the finger of God I drive out demons. (Luke 11: 20); 'by the Spirit of God...' (Matt 12: 28)*

'Then when I realised that since Healing was one of the nine extraordinary gifts of the Holy Spirit, *(1 Cor.12: 9 ...to another faith by the same Spirit, to another gifts of healing by the one Spirit),* I decided that we ought to start the workshop with *The Gift and Gifts of The Holy Spirit.*

The Holy Spirit's presence and activity in Jesus' life have not yet received the attention they once claimed in the early Church. For the past few centuries, the Church, and even some theologians today, have tended to look upon Jesus' baptism in the river Jordan as a minor episode in his life and therefore we miss the realisation that this was in fact a **major incident in Jesus' life.**

Cantalamessa points out that 'With the second Vatican Council, this mystery (of the anointing) has resurfaced in the Church's consciousness... The Holy Spirit's presence and activity in Jesus' life has not as yet, even in conciliar texts, received the attention they once claimed in the Church's theology...'[6]

So what is the significance of Jesus' baptism?

Cantalamessa drills down even further when he states that, 'The mystery of the anointing is like a sunken treasure, only now beginning to re-emerge on the surface. The Second Vatican Council drew up guidelines, indicated where to excavate. We must go back and excavate in the ground of the Bible and of the most ancient tradition of the Church but with the tools furnished by the latest exegesis and theology.'[7]

We begin to understand that at his baptism something happened that changed dramatically the course of his life (Luke 3:21-22). This is **not** new theology but based on the Bible and on ancient tradition.

Cantalamessa continues, *'At baptism something happened that modified the course of Jesus' life…We are entitled to suppose that this was the moment when Jesus accepted his vocation (C.H. Dodd)…It was at the moment of his baptism that Jesus must have acquired the certainty that he had to assume the role of the Servant of Yahweh' (O. Culmann).'*

Therefore for some years now this is how I started the Healing 1 Workshop.

**Here is a story you haven't heard before; we start with:**
Luke 3: 21-22; *'Now when all the people were baptised, and when Jesus also had been baptised and was praying, the heaven was opened, and the Holy Spirit descended upon him in bodily form, as a dove, and a voice came from heaven, 'Thou art my beloved Son; with thee I am well pleased.'*

When Jesus was praying, he received the fullness of the Holy Spirit, which empowered him to be **the Messiah.**

The voice of the Father in heaven quoting Psalm 2, one of several scripture references about the One who is to come, was telling Jesus that he was **the Messiah**, so he goes into the desert to pray to find out what his father wants him to do and it is the Holy Spirit who leads him into the desert to be tempted by the devil.

Then Luke 4:1-2; *'...and Jesus, full of the Holy Spirit, returned from the Jordan, and was led by the Spirit for forty days in the wilderness, tempted by the devil. And he ate nothing in those days; and when they were ended, he was hungry.'*

Which is **the first** of the 3 temptations? Very few people know which is first even if they know that there are three. The stones-to-bread is the first. *Why?* The devil always goes to your weak point; Jesus was hungry.

Now look at the last line of the temptations, verse 13 *'And when the devil had ended every temptation, he departed from him until an opportune time.'* When would this be? It would be at both Gethsemane, and on the cross, when Christ was at his weakest.

Then Luke 4:14 – 21 '...*and Jesus returned in the power of the Spirit into Galilee, and a report concerning him went out through all the surrounding country. And he taught in their synagogues, being glorified by all. And he came to Nazareth, where he had been brought up; and he went to the synagogue, as his custom was, on the Sabbath day. And he stood up to read; and there was given to him the book of the prophet Isaiah. He opened the book and found the place where it was written.*'

Isaiah 61: 1 '*The Spirit of the Lord is upon me, because he has anointed me to preach good news to the poor. He has sent me to proclaim release to the captives and recovering of sight to the blind, to set at liberty those who are oppressed, to proclaim the acceptable year of the Lord.*' *And he closed the book, and gave it back to the attendant, and sat down; and the eyes of all in the synagogue were fixed on him. And he began to say to them, 'Today this scripture has been fulfilled in your hearing.*'

**It is one story. However, we don't see it as one story because the Genealogy from Luke 3: 23-38**

**and the temptations in the wilderness Luke 4: 3-13 get in the way.**

What I do for small groups is give each one a photocopy of the two pages of my bible containing the above and give them either scissors or black felt pens and tell them to cut out or cross out everything before the baptism and the beginning of the public ministry at Nazareth (i.e cut out the genealogy and the temptations) and see what they are left with: **one story - even if it is in bits hanging together.**

Notice **the Holy Spirit is the connecting link.**

**Why have we never heard this story before?** Because we hear the story on three different occasions; about the Baptism on one Sunday in January, the Temptations in the Wilderness on the first Sunday of Lent, and Jesus reading the quote from Isaiah in the synagogue on the Third Sunday of the year in late January. However, no one seems to have put them together to form one story linked by the Holy Spirit.

To sum up - Jesus is baptised and receives the gift of the Spirit, which empowered him to be **the Messiah**, is led by the Spirit into the wilderness and returns in the power of the Spirit into Galilee, where he quotes from Isaiah 61 in the synagogue, saying he has been anointed by the Spirit to do all the things that the Messiah was going to do, *'Today this scripture has been fulfilled in your hearing.'* Therefore, in effect, he is telling the people in the synagogue **'I am the Messiah.'**

Did John the Baptist know that Jesus was the Messiah?

Luke 7: 18-23 John the Baptist in prison, sends two disciples to ask Jesus: *'…are you the one who is to come (the Messiah) or should we look for another?'* Among the experts there are two modes of thinking. The first is that John did not know that Jesus was the Christ and wanted to find out. The second is that John knew perfectly well, but his disciples were saying to him 'This chap you baptised, he's doing wonderful things among the people.' So John, in order to let his disciples see for themselves that

Jesus was the Christ, sends two of them. Jesus does not answer their question but puts on a show of healings and says: *'Go back and tell John what you have seen and heard…'* implying, I am the MESSIAH.

The Christ is the Messiah and is the Anointed One (by the SPIRIT) .

The definite article 'the' with the word Christ is very important. We English do not realise the importance, whereas the French do, because they always say 'le Christ'. For Christ is not a name. If it were, we would have Joseph Christ, Mary Christ and Jesus Christ. No, it is not a name, it is a function, like the butcher, the baker and…

Jesus Christ was **empowered** by the Holy Spirit after his baptism to do the job of being the **MESSIAH**. What was the job of being the Messiah?

The important phrase in Luke 4:14-23 – to describe the job of the Messiah - is **'to set free those who are oppressed,'** which applies to both healing and casting out evil (Healing Workshop 2). Using the

Holy Spirit, Jesus went round 'doing good.' In Acts 10.38 Peter preaching after Pentecost says:

*'...how God anointed Jesus of Nazareth with the Holy Spirit and with power;* **how he went about doing good** *and healing all that were oppressed by the devil,* **for God was with him.'**

The Gospels are full of: **preaching** the Good News, **healing** the sick and **casting out** evil. Whenever Jesus sends out 12 apostles or 70 disciples, it is always these same three things:

a) Preaching the Good News,

b) Healing the sick,
Matthew 9:36, *'...When he saw the crowds, he had compassion for them, because they were harassed and helpless, like sheep without a shepherd.'*
Matthew 14:14, *'...As he went ashore he saw a great throng; and he had compassion on them, and healed their sick.'*

c) Casting out evil.
1 John 3:8, *'The reason Jesus came was to destroy the works of the devil.'*

Mark 1: 27, *'What sort of new teaching is this?' they asked excitedly. 'It has such authority! Even the evil spirits obey his orders!'*

There are a multitude of verses in the bible about Jesus 'doing good'. In fact if you look at Mark's Gospel, on every page of chapters one to six you will find either a healing or a casting out evil.

Mark 10: 46 *'Bartimaeus, a blind beggar, the son of Timaeus, was sitting by the roadside. And when he heard that it was Jesus of Nazareth, he began to cry out and say, 'Jesus, Son of David, have mercy on me!' And many rebuked him, telling him to be silent; but he cried out all the more, 'Son of David, have mercy on me!' ...and Jesus stopped and said, 'Call him.'...and throwing off his mantle he sprang up and came to Jesus. And Jesus said to him, 'What do you want me to do for you?' And the blind man said to him, 'Master, let me receive my sight.' And Jesus said to him, 'Go your way; your faith has made you well.' And immediately he received his sight and followed him on the way.'*

***The Healing of the Blind Bartimaeus
by Harold Copping (1907)***
*Courtesy: http://truthbook.com/newsletter/
the-healing-of-the-blind-bartimaeus-painting*

## LOVE, FORGIVENESS, AND HEALING

HEALING is a vast subject covering a lot of ground. I'm not sure if it is generally known that there is scientifically proven natural healing which some people possess. I have seen heat photographs of a person's hand and arm before and after being held by someone else showing by means of colour, that the chemistry changes.

Our concern today is mainly about **Inner Healing** often called **Healing of the Memories** (when we allow **Jesus Christ** to bring back memories **which he wants to heal**). I only talk about Healing in relation to Jesus Christ - it's a spiritual thing, which needs a spiritual answer.

I do not use psychology, psychiatry or psycho-therapy although I was once told, having just given a talk on Healing in a parish situation:
'That was a very interesting talk Father. In it you used six therapies'
'Oh,' I replied. 'Did I?'
And I forgot to ask which ones!

I would suggest that every single person in the world could benefit from **Inner Healing** because we have all been hurt in our emotions in big or small ways. It seems to be part of ordinary living. Most of us can get by and live with our little problems, yet sometimes they become irksome or too big for us. Then they need healing and what surprises me is that it is so simple, so exceedingly simple that anybody, who is willing to pray and have a relationship with Jesus Christ and accept him as their Lord and Saviour, their Messiah, their God, and accept the power of the Holy Spirit in their lives, can pray for Healing.

Jesus himself says:
John 14:12 *'Truly, truly, I say to you, he who believes in me will also do the works that I do; and greater works than these will he do, because I go to the Father'*

Why does he add on the phrase *'because I go to the Father?'* He means: I go to the Father in order to send the Holy Spirit who will do all these things through you just as he did them through me.

John 15: 26 *'But when the Counsellor comes, whom I shall send to you from the Father, even the Spirit of truth, who proceeds from the Father, he will bear witness to me;'*

If only priests were trained to pray for Healing and Deliverance, so many more people would benefit.

---

## Witness Statement One

I am writing to you to say a very heartfelt thank you for the Day of Recollection on Saturday. It was wonderful to listen to you and you helped me to understand more about what God wants me to do with my prayers.

It's funny that when you were talking about the healing part in the afternoon, it suddenly came to me that the reason I have been having feelings of hatred towards my grandparents is because I was scalded with hot water when I was 3 years old and I have never forgiven my aunt and them, my grandparents, for letting this happen.

Since Saturday, I have prayed that I may let go of these feelings and know that I am starting my journey to forgiveness. I never would have come to this realisation if you had not allowed me to have a special contact with Jesus that day.

Hilda

---

Healing, as we are beginning to see, is God, who made us to *Love him, serve him and be happy with him forever in heaven* (Penny catechism when I was a boy) having compassion and mercy on us so that we may have a life full of joy.

John 15:11, *'These things I have spoken to you, that my joy may be in you, and that your joy may be full.'*

Matthew 14:14, *'As he went ashore he saw a great throng; and he had compassion on them, and healed their sick.'*

But what stops people believing in this joy and that Jesus has compassion on us is a mis-translation of the bible.

I want to mention the first commandment - it is long but the part I want to draw your attention to is:

Deuteronomy 5:8-10, *'You shall not make for yourself a graven image... you shall not bow down to them or serve them; for I the LORD your God am a jealous God,* **visiting the iniquity of the fathers upon the children to the third and fourth generation** *of those who hate me, but showing steadfast love to thousands of those who love me and keep my commandments.'*

Now that is the Revised Standard Version (RSV), which uses the phrase *'visiting the iniquity of the fathers...'*

As does The King James Bible and The New King James Bible and some other modern versions, which I prefer. Most versions of the bible, as far as I can ascertain, use the word *punish.*

*'...for I, **Yahweh** your God, am a jealous God and I **punish** the parents' fault in the children,'* (New Jerusalem)

*'...for I, the Lord your God, am a jealous God, **punishing** the children for the sin of the parents to the third and fourth generation.'* (New International)

*'...I bring **punishment** on those who hate me and on their descendants.'* (Good News Bible)

*'...and I put the **punishment** of the fathers upon the children, into the third and the fourth generations of those who hate me.'* (Wycliffe Bible)

*'I **punish** the children for the sin of their parents. I judge the grandchildren and great-grandchildren of those who hate me.'* (NIRV)

***'I hold parents responsible for any sins they pass on to their children to the third, and yes, even to the fourth generation.'*** (The Message)

I am reliably informed that 'punishing' and 'visiting the iniquity of the fathers' are accurate translations of the Hebrew. However, something has been lost in translation and my interpretation is that our God cannot punish the children, because it does not make sense when we are considering Healing by a God who loves us. I interpret the phrase *'visiting the iniquity of the fathers'* as meaning, when the parents don't want God, the blessings stop and the children lose out. I ask a member of a workshop 'Are you a millionaire?' expecting they will say 'No.' 'If your grandfather had been a millionaire, in normal circumstances you would now have some money, but because he gambled away all his money, you don't have any. Who do you blame, God or your grandfather?'

Yet, everybody blames God because the bible says: *punishing the children for the sin of the parents...*

## DEFINITION OF HEALING

**Inner Healing** is simply **God's love** flowing

through us, and as it flows, it **heals**. What stops his love from flowing through us is our lack of **forgiveness**.

**LOVE is the most important word**, more important than forgiveness, but forgiveness is needed in order to unblock the negativity or resentment in us so that we are able to love. It's the love, which does the healing. We will find out later how to love.

John 3: 16 *'...For God so loved the world that he gave his only Son, so that everyone who believes in him might not perish but might have eternal life.'*

Cardinal Hume gave a talk on prayer in Notre Dame Cathedral in Paris - his first sentence was: **'The beginning of prayer is the awareness that we are loved by God.'**
The important word is LOVE. Healing is simply God's love flowing through us.

## DO I LOVE MYSELF?

Most of us know that God loves everybody, but we

know it in our **heads.** I get a lot of people saying to me 'I know God loves everybody, but I'm not sure about me.' **The secret of life is to know deep down in my heart that God loves me.** Quite honestly, the only reason I can **love myself** is because I **know in my heart** that God loves me.

Ephesians 1:18 '... *having the eyes of your heart enlightened,'* so that we can see things the way God sees them. If only we believed what God says in the bible, we would begin to believe that God loves us.

Ephesians 1:19 '*...and what is the immeasurable greatness of his power in us who believe.'* There is a tremendous amount of God's power available to us that we do not use.

Why aren't we taught to use God's power and gifts?

To emphasise that God is always trying to give us gifts and to help the listeners to remember this, I draw a large letter **'S'** in the air, which they can read as S followed by a small letter s. They tell me that the latter is a 'small s,' so I ask them what is the large S, hoping to elicit from them the word 'largesse,' an English word derived from the French, defined as 'a generous bestower of gifts.' St Paul, in his letters, uses the words 'lavishly' or 'abundantly' to describe how God gives us his gifts. If only we were willing to accept what he tries to give us.

Ephesians 3:19 *'...to know the* **love of Christ** *which is beyond* **knowledge,***'* means knowing in our hearts that God loves us rather than just knowing in our heads (knowledge). The same verse continues: *'that you may be filled with all the fullness of God.'* There it is again, God is trying to fill us with his fullness.

We can see below the difference between 'head knowledge' and 'heart knowledge.'

John 4: 39 *'Many Samaritans from that city believed in him because of the woman's testimony, 'He told me all that I ever did.' (head knowledge for them) So when the Samaritans came to him, they asked him to stay with them; and he stayed there two days. And many more believed because of his word. They said to the woman, 'It is no longer because of your words that we believe,* **(head)** *for we have heard for ourselves, and we know (**heart**) that this is indeed the Saviour of the world.'*

I estimate from my experience that of the people I meet, either in groups, in the workshops, or as individuals who come to see me, at least 95% of them do not love themselves, do not know deep down in their hearts that Jesus loves them. **This is the beginning of the spiritual life.** Remember what Cardinal Hume said: **The beginning of prayer is the awareness that we are loved by God.**

We cannot go forward in the spiritual life until we accept Jesus into our lives. Paul tells us in 1 Cor. 12: 3 *'Therefore I want you to understand that no one speaking by the Spirit of God ever says 'Jesus be cursed!' and no one can say 'Jesus is Lord' except by the Holy Spirit.'* So in order to accept Jesus into our lives we need the **power of the Holy Spirit**. This will only happen when we begin to form a relationship with the Holy Spirit and with Jesus,

Pope Francis writes in *'Evangelium Gaudium'* -

*The Joy of the Gospel* - that we need a personal relationship with Jesus:

*'I invite all Christians, everywhere, at this very moment, to a renewed personal encounter with Jesus Christ.'*

He is saying that we need to have this relationship with Jesus so that we know deep down in our hearts that he loves us.

Jesus put this same idea to his disciples

Matthew 16:13, **'Who do men say that the Son of man is?'**
Luke 9: 18 **'Who do the people say that I am?'** They said,
*'John the Baptist; but others say, Eli'jah; and others, that one of the old prophets has risen.'*

And Jesus says to them **and to us as well:**

Matthew 16: 15 He said to them, *'But who do* **you** *say that I am?'*
Peter answers: **'You are the Christ, the Son of the living God.'**

And Christ commends Peter in v.17, *'Blessed are you, Simon Bar-Jona! For flesh and blood has not revealed this to you, but my Father who is in heaven...'* but 5 verses later, when Christ is saying that he must suffer and die, Peter says: *'God forbid, Lord! This shall never happen to you.'* Christ responds: *'Get behind me, Satan! You are a hindrance to me; for you are not on the side of God, but of men.'*

The contrast is vivid between verse 17 and verse 23 - one is a revelation from heaven and the second is speaking as a human being.

**And I myself want to answer with Peter *'You are the Christ, the Son of the living God.'*** For that is who Jesus Christ is for me, my God, my Saviour, my Redeemer, my Messiah who came to set me free.

## A TRUE STORY OF BEING MISTAKEN FOR SOMEONE ELSE

Now although I took my vows in 1955, I have taken another vow in the last 10 years or so. Whenever the gospel passage is about Christ asking his disciples *'Who do men say that I am'* and I happen to be preaching that day, I have made a vow to tell a story. My homily starts thus:

### Have you ever been taken for somebody else?

I had been asked to take over the parish of New Hartley, north of Newcastle in the North East for ten days until we gave the parish over to the bishop of that diocese, but although the bishop had earmarked a priest to go to New Hartley it could not happen immediately, so I stayed there for ten months. I went one day to have lunch with the parish priest of the neighbouring parish, a beautiful village called Cramlington, and what did the Housing Authorities do but build a new town right next door to the village, calling it Cramlington New Town. Of course all the roads were new, parallel to each other and others at right angles and whenever they crossed there would be a roundabout. As I left after lunch, the priest said to me 'Do you know the way?' and I, always being the expert answered: 'Yes, thank you,' and off I went up the main road intending to turn left at the first roundabout. This was blocked in order to keep the village as a village, so on I went to the next roundabout. However, before turning left I parked myself just before the turn and got out my special map. Why a special map? Well the Police, the Fire Brigade, the Ambulance Service had to have a special map of the area so they could find a place quickly.

As I was looking at my map and working out how to proceed, out of the left-hand turn came a Volvo. It went round the roundabout, the lady driver looking at me, and turned left in front of me, then reversed into a side road and repeated the operation once more passing by me, still looking at me, turning left as before and a third time came round and parked behind me.

**Now, how did my homily start?**

She came to my window and asked me, 'Are you COCO the CLOWN?' All I could say was 'No.'
'Oh' she said, 'I'm awfully sorry. We are having a

children's party and I saw you looking at the map and just knew you'd got lost.'

Then fortunately for me I remembered Jesus himself was thought to be mad:
Mark 3:21 *'...and when his family heard it, they went out to seize him, for people were saying, 'He is out of his mind,'* so I was in good hands.

We cannot go forward in the spiritual life until we accept Jesus into our lives, the Jesus who tells us that he loves us if we are prepared to listen. As Pope Francis says, *'I invite all Christians, everywhere, at this very moment, to a renewed personal encounter with Jesus Christ.'* I ask you, dear Reader, to try to answer that very important question **put to us** as well as to his disciples by Jesus, *'Who do **you** say that I am?'*

The following questions may help you assess your situation. Please answer the questions, by circling the Yes or No, straight away without thinking too much or at all.

# QUESTIONNAIRE

(circle your responses)

1. Do you find yourself needing approval from others to feel good about yourself?     Yes   No

2. Do you agree to do more for others than you can comfortably accomplish?     Yes   No

3. Are you a perfectionist?     Yes   No

4. Or do you tend to avoid or ignore responsibilities?     Yes   No

5. Do you find it difficult to identify what you're feeling?     Yes   No

6. Do you find it difficult to express feelings?     Yes   No

7. Do you tend to think in all-or-nothing terms?     Yes   No

8. Do you often feel lonely even in the presence of others?     Yes   No

9. Is it difficult for you to ask for what you need from others?     Yes   No

10. Is it difficult for you to
   maintain intimate relationships? Yes No

11. Do you find it difficult to trust
   others? Yes No

12. Do you tend to hang on to hurtful
   or destructive relationships? Yes No

13. Are you more aware of others'
   needs and feelings than your
   own? Yes No

14. Do you find it particularly
   difficult to deal with anger or
   criticism? Yes No

15. Is it hard for you to relax
   and enjoy yourself? Yes No

16. Do you find yourself feeling
   like a 'fake' in your academic
   or professional life? Yes No

17. Do you find yourself waiting
   for disaster to strike even when
   things are going well in your life? Yes No

18. Do you find yourself having
   difficulty with authority figures? Yes No

Most people could probably identify with some of the questions. If you find yourself answering 'Yes' to over half, you may need some healing.

*Suggested Prayer:* How to learn to love oneself:
*Lord Jesus, I NEED your gift of love deep down within myself, in my innermost being, so that I know that you love me, so that I can love you, love everybody and love myself.*

This prayer needs to be said often - 1,000 times a day?

We may have to force ourselves to love, because we have had a whole lifetime of doing the opposite. Remember, as I said before, I estimate that 95% of the people I meet do not love themselves, because they have no relationship with Jesus. This we will find difficult or impossible because we have not been taught the gospel, and because we have not been evangelised, we do not know who Jesus Christ is. Nowadays, Popes and Bishops are talking about New Evangelisation; what we in fact need is the

Old Evangelisation, or what is usually called the Gospel, pure and simple. This is the very point that Pope Francis, in *Evangelium Gaudium* (The Joy of the Gospel) urges us *'to a renewed personal encounter with Jesus Christ.'* He is saying that we need to have this relationship with Jesus so that we know deep down in our hearts that he loves us.

David Bates, a friend of mine, whom I baptised many years ago, and who currently lives in the US, writes a blog called *Restless Pilgrim*. In it, he narrates that when he was in England, visiting hospitals, as part of a prayer group, he met and spoke to many people and I quote a section from it.

---

## LOSING MY RELIGION
### *(Restless Pilgrim)*
### By David Bates

'Inevitably, we would end up spending much of our time talking to lapsed Catholics. We would regularly encounter those who didn't practice their faith and who hadn't entered a Church in years – they had been 'sacramentalised,' but not evangelised. Because they had received Baptism, First Holy Communion and Confirmation, they instinctively wrote down 'Roman Catholic' on their paper-work.'[8]

---

## HEALING OF MEMORIES

**Love is not a feeling; it is an act of the will. A decision.** If we find it impossible or difficult to love, we need **to forgive**, but very often we don't know whom we have to forgive because the mind tends to forget. So our prayer to God is to ask him to help us find out whom we have to forgive. Either pray by yourself or get people to pray with you (with the laying on of hands - an ancient gesture) as in:

Mark 5: 22, Jairus says to Jesus: *'My daughter is at the point of death. Please, come **lay your hands on her** that she may get well and live.'*

This prayer is sometimes called **Prayer for Inner Healing,** or **Emotional**, or **Psychological Healing,** but probably best of all it is called the **Healing of Memories**. My definition of 'Healing' is God's love flowing through me. As it flows it heals, and what stops his love from flowing is my lack of forgiveness. So what do I have to do? Find out whom I have to forgive. How? Pray, as we said above or the prayer below:

*Barbara Schlemon Prayer for healing.* This allows Jesus to bring back memories of hurts in the past. The problem is we human beings always want to be in control, so when we start using this prayer the human being in us immediately tries to remember, so we can tell Jesus what to heal - how stupid can we be? No, we have to force ourselves to go blank and let Jesus bring back the memories that **he wants to heal**. The dots are there for pauses of time (say 15 seconds) to allow Jesus to bring back a memory. Please remember that most of us do not like hurtful memories and we immediately dismiss them, push them back down inside us to fester. **No. Memories come back to be healed.**

### HEALING PRAYER
### by Barbara Schlemon Ryan[9]

We cannot repress hurts, sorrows and pains for long without them coming back either physically or emotionally. It is difficult to accept the love of Christ or receive the Holy Spirit, if we have accumulated hurts in our deep mind. These buried experiences make us keep our guard up, even against God, to be protected from further pain. We can pray for healing of these deep hurts in the following way:

'Lord, come into the deep heart of my mind. I want you to heal those things I have carried all this time. Take them to yourself. I can't carry them any more.'

Ask Jesus to walk back through our lives and heal us. Find a quiet place. Come before Him in humility and trust. Healing is an ever on-going process so all problems will not be solved; but we can get the big barriers out of the way. Inner healing is accomplished when a past event no longer has power to hurt us, when it can be recalled without sadness, shame or guilt. Begin by saying:

'Lord Jesus, thank you for being here, for your strength and presence. You can walk back through my life to the very moment when I was conceived. Help me even then; cleanse my bloodlines and free me from anything that may have caused difficulty before I was born, through my mother or circumstances... For this I give you thanks.

Heal me of the pain of birth. Thank you that you were there to receive me into your arms when I was born. Consecrate me in that moment to you ................ I thank you Jesus, for this has been done.

I praise you because in my infancy you were there when I needed love, needed to be held close, and comforted. Lord, do this in the depths of my being now................. Fill in that part of me that was neglected with strong fatherly love, security, and strength................... Thank you Lord Jesus for doing this.

Heal the part of my childhood that never felt wanted. Let me know that I am your child, a unique person in your family................ Thank you, Lord.

Heal me of hurt in family relationships. A brother or sister, who didn't understand, etc. Help me to reach out in forgiveness to them and accept them................... Thank you Lord for this that you have done.

Heal me of hurt in family relationships. A brother or sister, who didn't understand, etc. Help me to reach out in forgiveness to them and accept them................... Thank you Lord for this that you have done.

Heal me of wounds and unkindnesses that I sustained at school. Take my classroom suffering when I grew afraid to speak out because of ridicule or criticism........................... Open up that door in my heart; let me relate in groups to others, with confidence and courage to do what you call me to do.................. Thank you Lord; I believe this is being healed now.

Heal me of the experiences and fears I endured in adolescence. Transform all the things I did and had done to me so that I can no longer remember them with shame........................... Thank you Lord.

Heal me of difficulties in my vocation in life:
a) in marriage, hurts and sorrows...........................
b) in religion, loneliness..........................

Let me feel such strength of love pouring into me I will never again doubt that the path I am treading is the one you called me to. Thank you, my Lord.

Loneliness.......................... Rejection...........................
Abandonment.........................

Heal me of all these, of all hurts that I have suffered in various situations, of the wrong that I have done and the shame. Help me to forgive myself, and others. Put in me a new sense of strength and purpose. Let me be a living witness to you. As your love flows over me, I give you glory, Lord, because I know it is being done.'

Now be silent for ten minutes: let the Spirit of God do His healing work in you, emptying your heart of everything that is not of God. Let God refill your heart with his love.

----

---

## HEALING THE HIDDEN SELF
### By Barbara Schlemon Ryan[10]

Lord Jesus, I ask you to lead me back to the very beginning of my life on this earth. Through the power of your Holy Spirit, guide me to that moment in time when I was created through the physical union of my father and mother.

Touch my parents with perfect love and supply whatever may have been lacking in their union with one another so that my conception may be surrounded with a positive, affirming environment of healing light. Set me free from anything, which would have affected the development of my mind, that might impede my ability to walk with you, Lord Jesus.

I do praise and thank you for all the beautiful ways I was loved and affirmed during my growth within my mother. I am grateful for the parents you gave me and ask you to help me forgive them for the times when I did not perceive their love.

Lord Jesus, go back with me to that moment in my life when the process of birth first began in my life. Please relieve me of any pain I may have felt; let the gentleness of your touch quiet any fears I may have had.   Heal me of any complications associated with my birth.  I ask you to receive me into your arms, hold me close to your heart and fill me with courage and confidence in facing the world.

I ask you to walk back with me to my infancy, bringing the light of your Holy Spirit into the dark corners of my memory.  Heal me of any real or imagined rejection by my father or my mother during this stage of my development.  Help me to feel secure just as you were given security through the watchful presence of St. Joseph and may I recognise my need for warmth and tenderness of a mother's love by gifting me with your own mother, Mary.  Place me in her arms.

If my infancy or early childhood contained episodes of illness or pain, set me free from the ways in which this has marked my life. I give into your hands this entire portion of my existence, believing that through your infinite mercy, it will be brought to wholeness.

Lord Jesus Christ, go back with me to the time of my childhood and help me to overcome any resistance in me against becoming childlike again. Help me recapture the wonder and awe of the little child within me. If my own father was distant, rejecting or unaffirming, take me to your Father in heaven and fill the emptiness with strong fatherly love. Please bless all the members of my family and help me to see them with your eyes and if I harbour any resentment against any of them, give me your forgiving love that I may be set free.

Heal me of wounds I may have felt in the classroom, from teachers, from other children, from abuse, or shame, or embarrassment that still burns within me. Help me to feel your gentle touch absolving me from any sense of 'sin,' washing me clean, restoring my self-worth once again.

Lord Jesus, go back in my life to the period between childhood and infancy known as adolescence and begin to heal me of any hurtful memories of that time. Let the light of your Holy Spirit light up those areas in my deep mind that need to be cleansed and set free. Heal me of any guilt, shame, or embarrassment, of those times.

Set me free from feelings of rejection, of being excluded from groups, or of being teased or laughed at. There was often tension between myself, and my parents, so I ask you to touch those unhealed memories of arguments and misunderstandings, which caused pain between us. Help me to stop blaming others for my failures in life and begin to assume responsibility for my own behaviour.

Lord Jesus, I ask you to bless those areas of my adult life, which need to be transformed so that I may reflect your presence in everything I do. Give me the gift of faith to believe that you are aware of every facet of my existence. Give me the gift of trust so that I may leave myself in your hands since you will *'not break the crushed reed nor put out the smouldering wick.'*

There have been moments of pain in my adulthood, which sometimes make it hard for me to be open to you and to others. Please touch my broken heart with the love of your Sacred Heart. Give me in a spiritual sense, a real heart transplant. For you said: *'Come to me all you who labour and are heavy laden and I will give you rest.'*

Grant me a fresh infusion of hope so that I may believe, even when I don't see the evidence, that you are bringing goodness into my life. Thank you for all the ways your love is already enabling me to grow strong, so that Christ may live in my heart through faith and then *'planted in love and rooted in love, I may with all the saints have the strength to grasp the breadth and the length, the height and the depth and to know the love of Christ which surpasses all knowledge, and I may be filled with all the fullness of God.'* (Ephesians 3:16 - 19)

---

## Witness Statement Two

It was very good to see you on Saturday. I really appreciate that you joined us for the day of prayer.

I am sorry that it has taken me such a time to write to you with my account of the emotional healing that I experienced in the summer. The testimony relates to Saturday 25th and Sunday 26th July. Most of the detail I recorded in my diary at the time so as not to forget it.

I went to confession at the end of the Day of Renewal. You will remember I had said that I find it very difficult to trust people. You asked me about my childhood and I said that I was aware that I had experienced rejection by my mother. You then asked me to bring to mind an occasion when I had felt this rejection and to concentrate on the feelings that the event provoked. The event that I recalled was a gift being rejected, but the feeling that I experienced was of being dirty (although I did not name this aloud). You then asked me to remember the earliest age that I had felt this feeling. I tried to remember further back but I couldn't name an age to which the feeling related. You prayed for insight, praying in tongues and then told me to pray for healing at the age of 3.

At home that evening I prayed my penance, Psalm 51/52, which made me weep when I read it, 'wash me whiter than snow', how did you know that? I made an examination of conscience, asked for insight into why I had felt dirty, prayed off spirits of grief and asked for healing which didn't come.

The next evening I prayed much more simply as you had suggested, 'Lord, heal me of whatever happened in my third year of life.' I felt a gentle, insistent heat inside my back and through to my chest. Not overwhelming of itself, although cumulatively it could have overwhelmed me. I felt my muscles relaxing and un-twisting themselves but from the inside - there was no external heat source! I longed for the experience to continue. I felt joy. The feeling eventually receded; I'm not sure how long the experience lasted, maybe a couple of minutes.

In thinking why the healing came on the second request and not the first it made me realise that healing is God's act to be acknowledged, thanked and praised, an unearned gift that was not achieved by my work of examination of conscience. And now I notice two changes; the feelings of dirtiness are gone; difficult or shaming circum-stances can make me feel uncomfortable but dirti-ness as a feeling is not triggered each time something negative or confrontational happens.

Secondly, the feelings of murderous rage that difficult situations could produce are gone too.

Louise

When Jesus brings a memory back, we should immediately say: *'Thank you, Lord. Now Jesus, please walk back with me to the moment it took place and help me to forgive X with your forgiveness and help me to love X with your love.'*

What has happened is that we have blamed someone for hurting us (we all do it) whereas the hurt is already inside us from sometime back in the past.

Did you know that we always blame others? (Adam blamed Eve and Eve blamed the serpent!) I'm always right! Often, we take things the wrong way and so we feel hurt by someone whom we blame, **whereas they, the people who seem to be hurting us, are signposts from God telling us we need healing.**

I used to say most (about 75%), of our hurts were not intended to hurt us. What I am now saying is that you, my dear reader, will find it difficult to accept and believe, but over time my experience tells me that at least 95% of our hurts were unintended. To illustrate how we always blame others and get things wrong, I have the story of the pig.

## PIG

You have to think of a road like the one outside Douai Abbey, narrow, winding, with hedges. It is a summer afternoon and a gentleman is driving along with the window down and round the bend comes a car almost on his side of the road and he has to get right into the hedge and as the car goes by, the female driver shouts **'PIG'** and his reaction is to shout **'COW'**. As he goes round the bend he crashes into an enormous...

Reader - it may take you a moment to get this, it was an enormous PIG.

I teach what many people say you cannot do: it is possible to change somebody, provided your prayer is, *'Lord, change this person but start with me'*.

A few weeks ago I was sent this email:

## Witness Statement Three

...On the subject of healing families...you may remember my story...my dad has been a free-mason for 60 years...he has been a difficult person to get along with for the same period of time...it's not just me that feels this but also my mother and 2 brothers...After your workshop I prayed 'lord give my father a spirit of repentance...but start with me... give me a spirit of repentance first'...The Holy Spirit duly convicted me of some sins...the experience was not pleasant but not terrible either...The following week my father phoned me up, apologised for his behavior towards me and asked for my forgiveness!!...In all the time my family has known dad, he has never asked for forgiveness...the week after that, he phoned me up and asked me if he could come to church with me!!! ...Watch this space!

Kind regards in His name...

Bill

## PROCESS

### Lady in parish

A lady came to see me. She had worked in the parish for years and it had been good. Now, there was a niggle almost every day since a new parish priest had come.

So I asked, 'when was the last niggle?'

'Er, about ten days ago,' she said.

This is my process.

Close your eyes, go back ten days and let yourself feel the niggle. Don't try and work anything out but just feel it and ask yourself how old do you feel. Slight pause, then she says 'It's my mother,' and I ask, ' What is?' She says, 'When I hear the priest, I hear my mother' and I ask, 'Why blame the priest?'

If she allows Jesus to heal her when she was a little girl through forgiving and loving her mother, he will heal the relationship with the priest. It's not the priest who is causing the problem. He is called the

**presenting problem**, whereas the mother is the **real problem.**

### Jim and his American brother-in-law

Jim and his brother are working out their late father's estate - he died recently. They have a sister married in America, and it is the American brother-in-law on the phone to Jim, ranting and raving, 'Why aren't you getting on with this estate?' They are waiting for probate. Jim says, 'I feel terrible, what can I do?''

**So process** - Close your eyes; go back to the phone call and just feel what you felt then. How old do you feel? Slight pause. Six years old. Where are you, at home or at school? 'It's my father.' I, myself, cannot remember the rest, but my guess is that at the age of six, his father did something or said something that was unjust and it is still in him. When he hears the brother-in-law on the phone (the presenting problem), he hears his father (the real problem). So there is a need for him to forgive and love his father when he was six years old, such as: *Jesus walk back with me to when I was six years old and help me to forgive my father with your forgiveness and help me to love him with your love.* The brother-in-law on the phone is the **presenting problem** while the father is the **real problem**.

## Nurse's six-year old son

A District Nurse came to see me in March 2013. She and her husband were very tired because their six-year-old son was having terrible nightmares every night since Christmas Day when he had seen the news on television of Joanna Yates who had been kidnapped and murdered in Bristol. Not even knowing if she were Christian, I said to her 'all you need do is this; when he is asleep, both of you sit with him and put a hand on his head, shoulder or arm. His spirit, your spirits and the Holy Spirit are all together. All you need to say is 'Lord, we need some healing.' I also added, 'My guess is that something had happened early on in his life.'

The next week, she told me he had only had two nightmares and he himself said they were nothing like the previous ones. After that, no more nightmares were reported. After five weeks had gone by, she said: 'What he doesn't know and what you don't know is that when he was two years old, whilst I was washing the car, he got lost. We've no idea what happened but something did happen and the television news triggered off the nightmares.

To illustrate the **Healing of Memories:**

**Kay** came to see me once a month to talk about prayer, spiritual direction, the Sacrament of Reconciliation, etc. As she was leaving one day she said she was going to the swimming baths to learn to swim. I expressed my surprise, as she was a retired head teacher. When I asked why, she said she always panicked in water. I said, 'Sit down. Close your eyes, you are panicking in water. Just let yourself feel it. How old do you feel?' Short pause - 'eighteen months old,' she replied. 'Where are you?' I asked. 'I'm in the bath, Mummy goes to the front door to let Granny in and she doesn't come back.' As you can imagine, the water is rising, the taps are running, an obvious reason for panicking.

'Ask Jesus for his gift of forgiveness so that you can forgive your mother for the fright you had in the bath and his gift of love so that you can love your mother when you are eighteen months old.' She prays that prayer and off she goes.

Four or five days later, I receive a letter from her filling four sides of paper telling me how she had been to a retreat centre the next day where she had prayed with lots of tears and there was a lot of healing going on. She loved her mother but had always felt there was something not quite right in their relationship. There was no more room on the paper, however a little piece of scrap paper tucked in with the letter said 'How about this, I swam a length yesterday.' A month later, she was diving in. Another month and she was teaching old ladies to dive in. She told me that one day she was having a cup of coffee with the instructors who were saying that there were some people they were trying to teach to swim who would never be able to swim no matter what they did, and that 'you are one of them and we can't make out how you can swim.' When she told them that we had prayed, they said, 'Oh, phooey' They wouldn't believe her.

## Brown dress

In August 1976, I was giving a retreat. It was very hot. In fact that particular year has been mentioned often in recent times as one of the hottest. I was giving talks in the mornings and evenings and people were coming to see me in the afternoons. The third person one afternoon asked me if she could switch on the electric fire. I kept a straight face and said yes. I was in my (black monk's) habit and it was very, very hot.

We talked about prayer and in the middle of a sentence she suddenly stopped and said,
'That brown dress,'
'What brown dress?' I replied.'Well, when I was eight years old my mother made me wear this

brown dress to go to school in and I hated wearing it, so I wore my coat over it.'

I suggested she should ask Jesus for his gift of forgiveness, to forgive her mother for making her wear this brown dress which she hated and his gift of love to enable her to love her mother when she was eight. She then carried on talking.

Three months later, she came to see me at Douai Abbey and told me that since the day I had seen her, she hadn't been cold anymore. We realised that for the teachers, the children and for herself, she had to have a reason why she was wearing her coat. The obvious reason was that she was cold. She couldn't live with a conflict so the body went cold so that she could tell the truth. Once she found out, there was no need to be cold. By the way, the age of eight is significant for females, but I don't know why.

## Communion

I had been giving a talk on Healing at a Charismatic Day of Renewal, after which I was vesting, in preparing for Mass, when a lady asked to see me for a minute. She told me she was never able to approach the altar rails to receive communion without feeling physically ill. Sometimes she could get there, sometimes she couldn't. I asked her about her First Communion - it was good; about her childhood - yes it was good; and loved by her parents - yes. Then, as she continued talking her face was changing as the memory came back. She told me that when she was a toddler, about two years old, someone who was going to receive communion took her down to the altar rails and just at that moment, a lady nearby committed suicide, by cutting her throat, giving her a terrible fright. I asked her had she ever remembered this before? She said, No.

I told her to ask Jesus to go back with her to when she was two and ask for his gift of forgiveness for the lady who gave her the terrible fright and his gift of love for her. The whole thing took two and a half minutes. I haven't seen her since, but I guarantee she no longer feels ill when receiving communion.

## Novices and Stones

When I joined the monastery in 1954, I was one of eight novices. There were four the year before, and as the Novitiate lasts two years there were twelve of us. We did not speak very much with the community except three or four times a week. After lunch, we twelve would go outside and recreate as a group. My manual work in the afternoons consisted mainly of mowing the lawns and we had lots of lawns. Now Berkshire, as some of you will know, is full of stones on the surface and you may realise that it is bad for the stones to engage with the blades. So I had a brilliant idea. As we went out of a side door after lunch, there before us was a large lawn. I said, 'Hey, fellas, wouldn't it be a good idea if we spread out on this side of the lawn, walk across picking up the stones and put them in piles at the far side?' They said: 'No.'

I didn't realise for some thirty years what that response had done within my spirit and one morning after spending the previous evening talking with a parishioner about the nearly 350 emotions that we can have within us, I said after receiving communion:

'Lord, I need some healing,' and the memory came back about the novices and stones. (Healing of Memories). I went through the process of forgiving and loving the novices and thought that's now finished. Later that same year I was giving a talk on Healing to 250 religious, mostly nuns (men don't have emotions!) and I spoke about the novices and stones only to find that the left corner of my lower lip was quivering - the sign in me that I am still emotionally involved. I explained to the sisters what was happening. Of course I had to renew my forgiveness and love for the novices. Again a year later, I was giving a similar talk to religious and again my lip trembled, but not as much as previously, so I had to forgive and love once more. One of my workshop notes says: When you feel a healing taking place, this is the **beginning of the healing not the end**, so we have to continue forgiving and loving. It is a process rather than a completed action. We have to be people who are willing to forgive and to love as part of our way of life. Another note asks: Does God say *'I **have** forgiven you'* or rather *'I **am** forgiving you'*. *God is I am, and is always in a state of forgiving and loving.* That's his job.

I would like to introduce here a story that actually took place, but first I must introduce Mike Sarson, the founder of East West Organisation, in Reading, Berkshire, who treats those who have addictions. He has got me involved in giving talks and seeing people in Recovery from Addiction because he saw the benefits of my workshops in helping such people, so much so that he is arranging to make a video of Healing Workshops I and II. He has taken part in every one of my workshops. He is part of World Community for Christian Meditation (WCCM) and this organisation has a section dealing with the Eleventh Step of the Twelve Steps Programme used by such groups as Alcoholics Anonymous, the Eleventh Step being *Meeting God in Prayer and Meditation.* One day in November 2012, Meditatio, the outreach of WCCM, organised a day for Mike and myself at St Cassian's, Kintbury, where Mike spoke about Meditation and I spoke about Healing for those in Recovery. I said in my talk that it seems to me that having reached Meditation, (the Eleventh Step) people in Recovery have arrived at a plateau and that's where they stop. But there is a lot more to help them, such as Inner Healing or Healing of Memories and Deliverance. A gentleman who had been present phoned me in December, to ask if he could come and see me. He came. He talked about his childhood, his bad or non-existent relationship with his father. We prayed about Forgiveness and Love, prayed for Healing and a Prayer of Deliverance (see Workshop II). He phoned me in January 2013 - he had dreaded going home for Christmas but he had gone and everything had changed. I said: 'Praise the Lord.'

Just recently before my Healing Workshop I, I thought, rather than tell the group his story in my words, I would ask him for a few lines which would come directly from him. He sent me this letter:

## Witness Statement Four

Dear Nicholas

It is good to hear from you. Please find below a couple of words on my experiences before and after my meeting you.

I was born in Ireland in 1977, growing up in a country house in Tipperary with both parents two brothers and one sister. My father was a severe alcoholic and drug user who consequently suffered continuous bouts of depression, occasional rage, an unwillingness to support the family financially or emotionally, and frequent suicide attempts. My mother felt compelled to hold the family together and was very controlling and hysterical if we did not do as she said. My parents were continually at war with each other I was certainly my mother's favourite and this created intense jealousy on my father's part. I became a kind of love rival to him and from the age of 10, I can remember him locking me in the garage and beating me for no good reason. Worse was the psychological abuse which consisted of him continually telling me I was ugly, stupid, would never succeed in life, and constant threats to kick me out of the house if I told anyone about what he did. Consequently, by my late teens there was a complete breakdown in communication between us and we very rarely spoke directly to each other. I had a deep hatred for my father and eagerly anticipated his death. Conversely, I was bound to my mother very closely and I would not do anything without her consent first, for example she chose my college courses. Though she never said that she disapproved of my girlfriends, I always felt that I was betraying her by having them. Perhaps because of this, I had never had a mature long lasting relationship with a woman. Nor indeed could I sustain friendships of any kind. I had a deep distrust of all people and would feel suffocated by their interest in me and run away.

In November 2012, I attended a day retreat with you and Mike Sarson at Kintbury. I listened intently as you spoke on the healing of memories and how past hurts that remain unresolved, ie unforgiven, tend to dominate one's life. I could see that although I was in alcohol recovery and a daily prayer and meditator I needed to supplement theses spiritual practices with the your teachings.

In December 2012, after an exchange of emails, I visited you at Douai Abbey. Throughout the day, you guided me in a loving and gentle manner. The day consisted of many forms of prayer and discussion but the part I remember most vividly is when I spoke of various incidents in my childhood. We asked Jesus to be present there in the situation and to bless the person who hurt me as I asked God to help me let go of the resentment. I had been haunted by deep hate-filled resentments all my life. I learned that we cannot forgive, only God can, all we can do is let go of the resentment. In doing so, forgiveness follows. As the day went on, I already felt a new and quiet peace.

Three weeks later, I was given the opportunity to see this healing in action as I returned to the homestead in Tipperary for Christmas. On the flight over I had my usual intense fear and anxiety about going home to see my family. In fact up to this point, the most difficult thing I could imagine doing was being in the presence of my family. However, almost immediately upon entering the house, I noticed that the same heaviness and sense of dread had almost disappeared. I noticed that they hadn't changed at all, rather I had. I felt much less sensitive in their company. I always felt that Dad was waiting for an excuse to sneer and mock me but this time that sense simply wasn't there. I felt much less harrassed than ever before and had the most relaxing holiday in years. On my return, I was struck at how my mind was becoming more and more quiet. My family, rather my very painful memories of them, were slowly but steadily slipping away and being replaced by a new peace. I returned to Ireland again for the following Christmas and can only say that it was a miracle! My father and I were loving and affectionate throughout my stay. I was not even trying to be more loving and affectionate, it simply happened naturally and effortlessly. I also have a much healthier relationship with my mother now. There is now a healthy, loving distance between us, which does not mean I love her less, rather I'm now free to love her more. What a gift! My brothers and sister say I seem ten years younger and so much more approachable. My chronic fatigue has disappeared. My body shape, which was always extremely thin, is now filling out. I look much stronger and healthier. I feel much stronger and healthier too. I feel that I have been set free from a prison and can breathe fresh air for the first time. God promises to make us anew in Christ and I know that is what has been done to me. I look forward to attending my second session with you in the near future. Most remarkably of all, I look forward to visiting my family again in the summer.'

With much gratitude,

Jack

---

## Your Journey Through Life:
## Healing Our Memories
## by Fr. Peter deSousa[11]

'Children learn to walk through trial and error. They remember past mistakes, look beyond them and seek new ways of reaching their goals. If they did not remember their mistakes, they may be inclined to repeat them.'

All of us have memories, both happy and painful. Because we have suffered, we can empathise with those who suffer in similar fashion, comforting them with the same comfort we have received. Read 2

Corinthians 1:3-7. Let us befriend our memories rather than ignore, deny or run away from them. When you can share them with a loving spouse, they lose their sting.

I was never spanked or harshly scolded as a child at home. But once when I was ten, I was very rude to a servant who walked across the badminton court while I was playing, so that I missed scoring a point. My uncle who was my partner whacked me hard with his racquet. I was upset and humiliated. I complained to my dad who pointed out to me, that I had insulted a poor man who was my elder and could not speak back. I had failed to respect him and abused my position as his son. He gently suggested that I ask the man for forgiveness. I did so. Both the whack and the gentle suggestion had a salutary effect on me. In this memory there is no sting. It has made me compassionate.

But in buried memories that are unhealed, chronic anger, sadness, depression, fear, anxiety, shame or guilt may prevent us from functioning as loving persons. With a particular person like a nun; or a type of person, like a person in authority; or when to in a particular social setting, like being interviewed for a job or when I fail to achieve a goal, do I tend to react in a manner that is irrational? When someone speaks in a loud voice or finds fault with me, how do I react?

As you share your life story with a loving, caring spouse, about your childhood, adolescence or early adulthood, you may recall certain failures, reprimands, humiliations, rejections, losses, sad or hurtful memories that bring back a lot of negative feelings. As your spouse lovingly and respectfully listens with care and understanding, you are no longer alone and see yourself as precious and loveable.

Your spouse reassures you that you are loveable and precious, no matter how you may have behaved. Seeing yourself through his/her eyes, your self-esteem is restored. Like the prodigal son who saw himself through the eyes of his loving father, and experienced the warmth of his embrace and the celebration of home-coming, you too can turn a limitation into a celebration. So share the event, the way you felt devalued, the negative feelings you had about yourself (resentment, unworthiness, fear, anxiety, shame, bitterness, sadness, loneliness).

Your spouse reflects back your feeling to you as a way of empathising with you. You feel understood, comforted and valued. You belong.

Now take a look at those who hurt you and ask God for the grace to forgive them. Place them beneath the cross of Jesus and allow his precious blood to cleanse them. Hear Jesus pray: *'Father, forgive him/her for they know not what they do.'* Make his prayer your own. Ask your spouse to pray with you for a forgiving heart so that you may completely let go of any desire for revenge. You want to forgive those who hurt you as a true disciple of Jesus, so that you may also receive forgiveness in like measure.

If you are the one who hurt others, be reconciled in the sacrament of confession. If the person you hurt is alive and it will be beneficial to them, ask their forgiveness. If you need to clear their good name or make restitution, do so. Do not cling any more to guilt, but believe that the precious blood of Jesus is all-powerful to wash away the vilest stains of sin. Having been cleansed and emptied of all these negative sentiments, ask God's healing and Holy Spirit, to fill your emptied heart with charity, joy and peace, patience, understanding of others, kindness and fidelity, gentleness and self-control (Galations 5:22-23). Ask your spouse to pray with you earnestly so that the fruit of the Spirit may make you a more loving spouse and parent. There are many memories in all of us that need healing and many of them are in the subconscious.

God gives spouses and parents the grace to heal. So avail of this grace. It is God who heals. Who can be closer and more intimate with you, than your spouse? You are called to be naked and unashamed with each other, not just physically, but also spiritually and emotionally. You are called to make a total gift of yourself to each other. So when husbands and wives share with each other in a vulnerable way, they build up trust between them. They can express their healing love intimately in a conjugal embrace, which one cannot do with a holy person who prays over you. Jesus is in your midst, as you heal in his name.

Likewise, children are the personification and fruit of conjugal love. Parents can embrace a son or daughter between them and listen with love to their fears, hurts and cry for healing. That parental embrace is healing and restores a son or daughter who has gone astray or is in need of healing. This is true even of adult children. Physical, emotional and spiritual healings accompany one another. It is Abba Father who heals and who shares the gift of parenthood with you. Allow him to do so.

Many marriages and homes are unhappy, because of alcoholism, addictions, nagging, lack of respect, no deep communication between spouses or between parents and children, lack of forgiveness, strained relationships, coldness, sarcasm, mistrust, suspicion and chronic illnesses. All these flow from buried anger, fear, guilt or anxiety. Where there is prayerful sharing, healing and reassuring love, these same homes will be transformed. Walk humbly with your God and with one another and you will be able to share the peace of Jesus with each other everyday. Healing of memories brings peace to the home and all who dwell therein.

## HOW DID I BECOME A PRIEST?

I am sometimes asked how did I become a monk and a priest.

After school, aged 18, I did two years National Service in the Army followed by three years working in London for the same insurance firm as my brother. It was a big company with its own luncheon club to which we went every day. It was a self-service canteen and the tables were cleared and cleaned by ladies one of whom was an Irish lady, Mary Flynn, who knew that my brother and I were Catholics *'by the look in our eyes!'*

One day, as I was leaving the luncheon club, she stopped me by the door and said, 'I saw you smoking your pipe just now. Did you ever think of becoming a priest?' I burst out laughing and said, 'Good heavens no, never, even when we had talks at school about vocations.' She never, ever, mentioned it again.

During the next two years the thought of becoming a priest kept coming back to me stronger and stronger every few weeks. I didn't know what to do so I applied to spend a year at Campion House, in Osterley. Having made a decision about what to do, I went home on holiday but I could not tell my mother. It did not make sense. I was timid and shy and no way could I tell my mother. However, I could tell my big sister, who is the eldest of five whilst I am the youngest. She is now 97 years old. What did she do? She told my mother, of course, who was baking in the kitchen. My mother appeared in front of me whilst I was reading the newspaper and holding her floured hands up in front of her she said, 'Son, how on earth are you going to be able to preach?' I did not know for about twenty years what that did within my spirit. After I was ordained I used to hate preaching, without realising why.

Then God, who always does things in the simplest way, got me involved in Charismatic Renewal in August 1975, which changed my life. It was then I knew what preaching was all about - Christ was the Messiah - Christ died and rose again. It is all so simple.

Now I take you back to near the beginning: Here is a story you haven't heard before.

Jesus was empowered at his baptism by the Holy Spirit to become the Messiah. He trained his disciples to preach the Good News, heal the sick and cast out evil. He returned to His Father in heaven, His work on earth accomplished, in order to send down the Holy Spirit on the disciples (Pentecost) so that they, and every Christian, could do as He had done: preach the Good News, heal the sick and cast out evil with the very same power of the Holy Spirit. What could be simpler?

Charismatic Renewal is no more than a personal awareness that Jesus Christ is my Saviour, my Redeemer, my Messiah, who wants to set me free. I was introduced to Charismatic Renewal and the Ministry of Healing about the same time - they are in fact very closely linked, certainly in the Catholic Church. As far as I can see, many people in the Ministry of Healing started in Renewal as I did.

## The Story of the Mother who phoned the Bishop

This story appears in the next workshop - Healing Workshop II on Deliverance. It is the story of a mother, called Maria, who phoned the bishop.

For four years before I met Maria, there was a lot of evil from her divorced husband both against herself and the two daughters. Maria came to see me and her terrible life up to that point changed through Prayer for Healing and Deliverance to one of serenity. We had talked about forgiveness and love and we ended with a prayer for healing and a prayer of deliverance and I anointed her. This specific story is not about Maria; it is about her daughters.

One daughter, Chantelle, weighed 17 stone when I met her. The other, Linda was slim. They came to see me with the mother and again we talked about forgiveness and love as I had done before. We ended the same way with a prayer for healing and a prayer of deliverance, all three being anointed. I knew Chantelle would find it extremely difficult to forgive her father who had sexually abused her from the age of six to twelve, but next morning she sent me an email saying 'Breakthrough. I am able to forgive my father. I have spent a lot of money on psychotherapy, and my psychotherapist tells me just what you tell me, but she says I have to do it, whereas you say Jesus does it for me - and he does.

She wrote a letter to me.

---

## Witness Statement Five

8th March 2009

Dear Fr. Nicholas,

I am writing to tell you of my experience with you. I first visited you about 18 months ago with my mother and sister. Our family, as you know, had been left in ruins after a very nasty divorce and annulment of my parents' marriage and when I realised I had been abused by my father as a small child. My relationship between my sister and my mother and I was fraught. I suffered with unpredictable sleep patterns, chattering in my head making it very hard to pray or meditate. I was haunted by the memories of the past and I was being attacked on a mental and energy level by my father.

My health was a mess and I was desperately over-weight to the point where I was risking developing Diabetes and heart problems. I did not care for myself. I did not love myself. I did not know that God loved me.

I had spent a lot of money on very good therapists who were unable to help me. Trying to explain to health professionals that you are not possessed but being attacked by evil spirits is impossible without risking being sectioned by a doctor.

When reading the Gospel so often did Jesus cast out devils and evil spirits from people, but people now assume that it is a problem of mental health and chemical imbalances and want to subdue it with pills rather than apply the correct spiritual cure for the problem.

My biggest issue was finding a way to forgive my father for what he had done. I had been told by priests in Lourdes, priests here in the UK, Victim Support, doctors and my therapist that I must forgive him otherwise I would carry the problem with me like a yoke around my neck for the rest of my life. None of them told me how. It is like saying to a 2-year old child, learn nuclear physics. It is not an easy thing to do at all even if you really want and no one seemed to know how when I asked them.

You were clear and exacting when you told me 'To err is human, to forgive is divine! It is not your job to forgive and you can't if you are human. This is Jesus' job to do it for you.'

You guided me in prayer and suddenly like a light being switched on I was able to truly feel the freedom that comes with forgiveness...

Chantelle

---

The other daughter had no problems, or so I thought. I did not yet know that the father had never spoken to Linda. Her mother told her to email me, which she did. She told me that she would go to work, switch on the computer and stare into space. Eventually the mother told me that Linda could never have any relationship whatsoever with any male. So I suggested praying with Maria as proxy for her daughter which we did - and not long after I had a visit from Maria, her daughter Linda, and her granddaughter Grace, six months old, who could not stop smiling at me. A miracle baby!

Linda married in America and had just come home for a visit. It was lovely to see the effect of prayer for healing and deliverance in a very practical way. I cannot stop praising God for the wonderful ways he has of answering prayer.

It is so easy to forget that God does the healing, not us. I think one of the worst problems in our lives is being human. The human being in us always wants to be in control - always. I take you back to Ephesians 1:19 *'...and what is the immeasurable greatness of his power in us who believe.'* I would suggest that this power is really the ability to get out of the way and let God do it, because the human being in us does not want to let God do it. It seems to me that all my sinfulness is my saying to God: *'my way is better because I want to do it my way.'* So here's a story to illustrate this.

## Christine and the freezing fog

Christine, a member of the Grail (a community of ladies, who translated the Psalms into English for singing, after the Vatican Council) was asked to go to Preston, in the north west of England, to open a new house. Whilst there, she was asked to give a spiritual talk. So off she went down the motorway, winter, freezing fog. Whenever she drove, she prayed - this time her prayer was 'Lord, I will arrive late, I'll be like a wet rag and won't be able to give your talk properly, so please take over the driving.' She kept hold of the steering wheel. She arrived early, fresh as a daisy and said to the Lord, 'You must like driving.'

He answers, 'I do, but I never get the chance!'

I once told this story to the group following the Life

in the Spirit Seminars. After the talks we go into groups to discuss what we have heard. I was in a group. The next week one person was missing from my group but returned the following week. As we went into our groups he said to me 'Father, it works.' I had no idea what he was talking about. He said, 'Yes, you know the story about Christine and the freezing fog. Well, I'm an airline pilot and as we are landing, I say, 'Lord, take over the driving' and he does!'

So let's give God the chance to do something in our lives.

---

### Witness Statement Six

[From Sandra, who brought her friend Helen, who she thought would be helped by a visit to me.]

Email: Thank you for giving Helen so much time on Monday; she seemed to benefit instantly. I also learned a lot just by being there. Perhaps she will come to one of your sessions on Meditation in Recovery, but I feel she may get called to Iran again soon.

*Email: 9 days later:*

I had very good news from Helen. The day after we visited you she spoke to her parents in Iran and several things happened: their kitten had been stuck in the air-conditioning ducting for three days and her father could hear it meowing as his hearing is so intense after losing his eyesight: The day you prayed with Helen all the neighbours got together and managed to cut into the ducting and freed the kitten – this overjoyed her father, but also as it took all day to do, it meant that all the neighbours who had feuds and problems between them got together for the first time and buried their grievances. Then for the first time in ages her mother laughed. And finally, the biggest thing of all - for the first time in her life Helen's father told her he loved her!

Sandra

---

Now tell me God doesn't help us?

## Medical conditions

Having learned about both Charismatic Renewal

and Healing, I looked in our Library at Douai but could find nothing on either subject. I then went to the Library in Reading, again nothing except I did find four books written by doctors in the early 1900's all saying the same thing. In those days, doctors said they could not cure four conditions but believed that 80% of conditions like backache, skin rash, arthritis, and migraine were due to resentment.

That I now presume was what started me thinking of forgiveness and love, for resentment is negative and stops us loving. Looking back I now see that in my first workshop, Healing 1, I spent most of the time talking about forgiveness.

## Back-ache

But it wasn't all theory! I have had severe back-aches, and I have had skin rash for two years. So I asked myself was I in the 80% or as I say to the people attending my workshop, don't worry if you have any of these four ailments, you could well be in the other 20%! Of course, I was in the 80%, but I did not know it at the time. What brought it to light was my severe backache in 1970. I was sent to an Osteopath for a two-hour session. After one hour he was feeling the vertebrae and he asked me had I had any accidents, car, bicycle, or horse. I said no, I had never had any accidents. 'Well,' he said, 'you have been concussed with your head turning slightly left.' 'Oh!' I said, 'Have I?' He continued the treatment and at the end of the next hour as I was about to leave I asked him if I could still take games, rugby, soccer, cricket, and he answered 'Give it ten days and you'll be fine.' At that very moment, I remembered having been knocked out playing rugby, during a game with monks and the boys, by one of my brethren, coming at me with his forearm and hitting me on the chin with my head in the direction indicated by the Osteopath. That was back in 1958.

But that is not all. In the 1960's during Vatican Council II, Rome suggested that monasteries like ours should have discussion groups. We had one, and after I had spoken, I was very firmly put down and I would not speak in a group again for five years. Who was that person? The very same person who knocked me out in the rugby game. My experience since then is that it is quite common for a hurt to be followed by ripples which again lead to more hurts and the situation can become quite negative, particularly in a family.

Of course, I did not realise at that time about forgiveness and love. It was some years later when I started the workshops that I realised the necessity of forgiving and loving. The same, of course, will apply to the following stories.

**Skin rash**

I had skin rash for two years, trying eight or nine different ointments to no avail. I had worked very amicably with Fr. Anthony for four years at our Prep. School at Ditcham Park, near Petersfield, Hampshire. In July 1975 we closed Ditcham and brought 40 boys back to Douai. Fr. Anthony became headmaster of the Junior School and I worked with him, but now it was not amicably. He knew something was wrong and suggested we talked, which we did but nothing came of it. Two years later, whilst I was giving a talk on Healing, my thought process was 'Nicholas, you are a chump, here you are telling the people what to do and you have not done it for yourself!' So on the way home, I asked the Lord why have I got this skin rash. He gave me two memories to do with Fr. Anthony (oh, so trivial) and once I had gone through the process of forgiving and loving him, the skin rash ceased except for one small part - to remind me to go on forgiving and loving. Then that ceased. Fr. Anthony knows the story.

## Arthritis

I didn't think I had had Arthritis but I have had two hips replaced and the suggestion was osteo-arthritis in both cases. But my story is slightly different. A lady Chiropractor and her husband came to one of my workshops and told me at the end of the day that they could help me. 'Come and have a meal and a session they said.' Being a little sceptical I did nothing until she phoned me and said in a voice, which would not accept a refusal, 'When are you coming?' So I went, had a very nice meal followed by a session, she asking me lots of questions while her husband was taking notes. At one point I said that I had arthritis in my left thumb. 'Why do you think you have arthritis in your left thumb?' I answered that my sister has this pain in one of her thumbs and was told it was arthritis and I have a similar pain. She told her husband to write it down - self-diagnosed arthritis in the left thumb - it is probably still in the notes.

## Migraine

I have never had a migraine.

## FORGIVE IN ORDER TO LOVE

*Only love will save us... Only love... for my Christian friends, and for my friends of good will but of no faith, (and unsure faith)... you all are beloved of God because your hearts are good.*

Quotation from Our Lady of Fatima:

We are all loved by God, everyone without exception, even the worst sinners, are all loved by God. As we saw earlier in **Do I love myself?** Most of us know in our **heads** that God loves everyone but it is theory, second-hand knowledge since we have been told by parents and teachers. We have to allow ourselves to know that God loves us, first-hand, directly from the source, that is God, who is love.

1 John 4:16 *'So we know and believe the love God has for us. God is love, and he who abides in love abides in God, and God abides in him.'*

How do we know directly from the source that God loves us? – Only through prayer, only by letting God himself tell us deep down in our hearts, in our innermost being. Only then we will **KNOW** in the same way that the Samaritan people who invited Jesus to stay with them **KNEW** in their **hearts** that he was the Saviour of the world.

I mentioned Mike Sarson earlier. He took me once to a Primary School where he teaches Meditation. The Headteacher had given a questionnaire to the children to find out what they felt. They all said things like 'I feel calm, I don't need to get angry, but if I do, it doesn't last long.' One seven-year old boy wrote: *'I just sit there and let God in'* That I think is very profound. That's what we need to do - *let God in*. He does the rest. You will realise that what I have been saying here is exactly the same as I said earlier from Pope Francis in his *The Joy of the Gospel* – *'I invite all Christians, everywhere, at this very moment, to a renewed personal encounter with Jesus Christ.'*

I repeat the prayer I gave you after the questionnaire:

**Suggested Prayer:** How to learn to love oneself:
*Lord Jesus, I need your gift of love deep down within myself, in my innermost being, so that I know that you love me, so that I can love you, love everybody and love myself.*

To be said often – perhaps a 1,000 times a day?

I am emphasising this necessity to **KNOW** that we are loved by God because otherwise we will never fully understand Healing, because Healing is simply God's love, **which we have experienced**. We just **know** it.

So let me again give you my definition of **Healing. Healing** is simply **God's love** flowing through us; as it flows it **heals;** what stops his love from flowing through us is our lack of **forgiveness**. I would suggest that lack of love is always the cause of a problem thereby needing forgiveness followed by love.

Now **Forgiveness** is important, not because it heals, but because it is the instrument, which unblocks us, to enable us to **Love** and it is the **LOVE** flowing through us, which heals.

So as we say the Lord's Prayer, we say: *'forgive us our trespasses as (in the same way as) we forgive those who trespass against us.'* We are in effect saying to God, don't bother to forgive me because I don't want to forgive the person who hurt me. It **should** seem to us illogical (but often doesn't) that the other person is not hurting, while I am hurting, because I am not forgiving, and who is the only person who can get rid of my hurt? ME! - by asking God to help me to forgive.

**The Father forgives the Prodigal Son
- by Rembrandt van Rijn (c.1669)**
*Courtesy: Hermitage Museum, St Petersburg, Russia.*

When you look at Matthew 6 where he gives us that prayer by Jesus himself, as he finishes: '*...and lead us not into temptation but deliver us from evil,*' he continues '*...if you do not forgive, neither will your heavenly Father forgive you.*'

IT IS NOT CONDITIONAL. It sounds conditional but it cannot be, for God's forgiveness and love cannot be conditional. It is all so very free. No, we are blocking God from forgiving us. What he wants us to do is; *as the Lord has forgiven you, so must you also do.*

Colossians 3:12-14, '*Put on then, as God's chosen ones, holy and beloved, heartfelt compassion, kindness, humility, gentleness, and patience, bearing with one another and forgiving one another, if one has a grievance against another; as the Lord has forgiven you, so must you also do.*'

Mark 11:25 '*When you stand to pray, forgive anyone against whom you have a grievance, so that your heavenly Father may in turn forgive you your transgressions.*'

Luke 6:37, *'Judge not, and you will not be judged; condemn not, and you will not be condemned; forgive, and you will be forgiven;'*

These last few scripture references - are they suggestions or are they saying, if you don't forgive, God cannot forgive you? Or are they commands? Read them again. If they are commands, then forgiving must be possible, because God could not command us to do something that was impossible. Being unable to forgive does not allow one to love and therefore, it is the greatest obstacle to holiness.

You remember in Matthew 18:21 Peter asks Jesus: *'How often do I have to forgive someone, seven times?'* *'No,'* says Jesus, *'but seventy times seven.'* That is a lot.

Again in Matthew 18:35 the unjust steward who had been let off 10,000 denarii by his master but would not forego the 10 denarii owed to him by a fellow steward *'And so will your heavenly Father do to you, if you do not forgive your brother from your HEART.*

It isn't that God doesn't want to forgive us, he does, but we block him from forgiving or loving us with our lack of forgiveness.

You remember Chantelle wrote:

*'...My biggest issue was finding a way to forgive my father for what he had done. None of them told me how. It is like saying to a 2-year old child, learn nuclear physics. It is not an easy thing to do at all even if you really want and no one seemed to know how when I asked them.'*

It is certainly not an easy thing to do, though there are degrees of difficulty depending on the type of hurt; You brush someone's shoulder in a crowd and you say 'Sorry, please forgive me'; your best friend abandons you; your spouse walks out on you; your son or daughter is murdered. God is still asking us to forgive and it can seem impossible to forgive. We saw that God could not command us to do the impossible, so forgiveness is always possible no matter how difficult.

At one and the same time,
Forgiving is the hardest thing in the world and the
easiest.
It is the hardest because we don't want to;
It is the easiest when we let Jesus do it.

## HOW TO FORGIVE

A little boy was asked: 'What is God for?'
The answer was:
GOD is for giving... I'm still trying to work it out!

Psalm 138(129), verse 4,
*'But with you is found forgiveness: for this we revere*
*you.'*

**'To err is human; to forgive is divine.'**
Alexander Pope

This tells me that forgiveness like love is a divine
gift. We cannot of ourselves forgive or love.

So how do we forgive? Don't try and feel it. **Do it.**
It's an act of the will, a decision. It's very important

to realise this. People want to have this warm feeling that they are able to forgive. No, it's a cold decision to ask God to do the forgiving or loving through us - he does it, not us. The warm feeling comes afterwards when we are set free. Remember, he does it.

-------------------

## To Err is Human; to Forgive, Divine
## by Fr. Peter deSousa[12]

Because we are all human beings, we can expect to make mistakes and at times slip back into selfish and sinful behaviour. Some of us may have rather poor self-control, when we are tired, stressed out or sick. But the other members of the family have a marvellous chance to show us God's forgiving love at such times.

When I was 9 years old, I quarrelled with an older sister and decided not to speak to her again since she was cleverer than me and would always win. My mother, who observed this, asked me if I wanted to live as God's child. When I said yes, she told me that God is a forgiving God, and if we want to live as his children, we have to be willing to forgive over and over again.

This made a deep impression on me. I often find it hard to forgive someone who is ungrateful, takes advantage of my kindness, makes use of me or a fool of me. My ego is threatened. 'Forgive us our trespasses as we forgive those who trespass against us' is a challenging prayer at such times. Jesus on the cross praying: 'Father forgive them for they do not know what they are doing,' brings me to my senses. In the measure that I forgive, I am forgiven.

I remember my Dad singing to my Mum, after a small tiff: 'Let bygones be bygones forever; we'll fall in love, once again.' Yes forgiveness is one of the greatest ways of loving and showing that we are Jesus' disciples. Husbands and wives, Parents and children, siblings are very human and all can act rather selfishly at times. Yet as disciples of Jesus, we have no option, but to forgive 70 times 7 times, which is without limit. How do we get this grace? Humble yourself before God and invite the Holy Spirit to soften your hard heart. I know of a couple who would lie prostrate before the

Blessed Sacrament and not arise until they were willing to forgive. It took 45 minutes at times, to let go of the other's offence.

In many homes, each one wants to win by making the other lose. I may enjoy being right, dominating the other, taking my revenge, teaching the other a good lesson, for a while. The other will feel resentful. After a while, my victory will be short lived too because we are out of relationship. If each one feels listened to and their feelings acknowledged, a solution is often found. So there are two factors to consider:

- The actual problem to be solved and
- Your relationship.

The second is more important.

1. Do not blame the other for your feelings: e.g. 'You made me angry.' Rather say 'I feel upset when you spend more than... on new clothes, without consulting me.'

2. Accept that this is how the other is feeling. Feelings are neither right nor wrong in themselves. Give feedback as follows: 'You feel upset when I

spend more than ...on clothes, without consulting you.' When both feel listened to and accepted with respect, it is easier to look at alternatives, weigh the pro's and con's and consider possible solutions.

There are various ways of dealing with conflict:
a. Saying nothing but sulking and avoiding the other
b. Abuse or violence
c. Acting the martyr and giving in with disgust or self-pity
d. Manipulating and bribing
e. Compromising (give and take), and
f. Collaborating - working out what is best.

What is your pattern? Share it with your spouse. Everyone has a family history where we learned how to deal with anger. Free yourself from the past and choose to modify your behaviour with the help of the Holy Spirit.

What are some areas where there is conflict and how can you resolve it? Agree on some ground rules of what is acceptable in your family. e.g. Using the phone. Bathroom occupation. Watching TV. Meal attendance. Noise level. Bed time.

Have regular times for reconciliation, resolving conflicts, listening, sharing and praying together before making major decisions. One family chose Fridays before dinner, when they reflected together on Jesus on the cross forgiving us. Alternately, read and reflect together as a family on Luke 15: 11-32 or Matthew 5: 1-12.

When we reflect back on our own personal history, we may recall past hurts that are still not resolved and bring back buried feelings of resentment, hatred or anger.

a. Bring Jesus into that situation and see yourself through his eyes. Allow him to love, comfort, strengthen and provide you with what you needed at that moment.

b. See those who hurt you through Jesus' eyes. Maybe Jesus was angry at the way they treated you and takes a whip to drive them out of the temple of your body or spirit, which they violated. But place them also under his cross and hear him praying to Abba Father to forgive them. Let his precious blood flow over them and over you.

c. Choose to consciously give up your resentment, fear, anxiety, shame, revenge or hatred. Cast it out from you with the power of the Holy Spirit.

d. Ask the Holy Spirit to fill those vacated areas of your life with love, joy, peace, kindness, gentleness, patience, praise and thanksgiving. Then those painful memories from your past are healed and you are free to love and forgive, as Jesus' disciples.

Married couples can do this prayer exercise with each other and take the part of Jesus to each other in listening, responding, embracing and healing the other. For this is the meaning of your sacramental relationship, to redeem and heal your spouse. The best place to do this is in your bedroom. Jesus wants you to listen, share, forgive and heal each other through his precious blood and his healing, life-giving spirit.

Parents can also heal their children by inviting them to come and lie down between them and share their hurts and frustrations. Silently listen to their feelings without defensiveness. Ask forgiveness if you have hurt them. Give forgiveness if they have hurt you. Help them to give up what negativity they are clinging on to and ask God's spirit to fill them with new life. Friends of mine healed their 31-year old son in this way. Try it. It really works. God gives you the grace to be life-giving to your children, not only in conceiving them, but always. Parents are the best healers of their children.

———————

If you remember a particular hurt and you know who hurt you, ask Jesus **to go back with you to the moment** when it happened.

**Suggested prayer:**
Lord Jesus, I *need* your gift of forgiveness to forgive $X$, with your forgiveness.
Lord Jesus, I *need* your gift of love to love $X$, with your love.

I add with your forgiveness, etc., to remind ourselves it is not ours but Jesus' gifts of forgiveness and love.

You may also use your imagination. Imagine Jesus

present with you - at that time. Does he say or do anything? I once had a forty-year old lady with several problems. I asked her which was the greatest hurt in her life. She said, 'When I was about thirteen, my father used to beat myself and my sister with his belt. On one occasion I had run into the kitchen and had fallen over and my father was standing over me with his belt ready. This image has haunted me all my life.'

I told her to use her imagination and imagine Jesus somewhere in the kitchen and told her to tell me: 'What does he do? What does he say?'

After a pause she said 'Jesus comes over to me, helps me up and takes me to my father, helps me put my arms round my father's neck and I say to him, father I forgive you and I love you.'

Her whole being changed; she was a different person. She knew she was a different person who could now love her father, no more shame, no more guilt, no more hurt. She was able to love.

Since many hurts happen in the family, see the 4th commandment   Exodus 20:12, Deut. 5:16 *'Honour your father and your mother, that your days may be long in the land which the LORD your God gives you.'*

No matter how well or badly our parents have treated us, God asks us to forgive them, for our own sake, for our own health, both physical and spiritual. Here is a story from George.

---

## Witness Statement Seven

I was a student at Douai School in the 1960s and after I left, I used to visit the Abbey and the school every few years. Although Fr. Nicholas was at Douai during my time, I only got to know him in the mid-1990s when he made me a wooden crucifix; the cross was made of mahogany, while the body of Christ was in the shape of a chalice and the head in the shape of a communion host, both made of light coloured wood. I have it to this day and admire its artistry.

It all started on a Friday night in February 2013, when I was depressed about my brother-in-law's treachery, which had unleashed an angry rage in me. I had been nursing it for months and it gave me a strange kind of warmth, but then left me with a bitter taste. I was unable to let it go and it was causing me immense grief. From previous visits to Douai, I knew about Fr. Nicholas' Healing workshops, so I decided then and there, to go first thing in the morning to talk to him.

The following morning, I arrived at Douai at 10:10. As I entered the lobby, there was a notice on the wall that read 'Healing Workshop III – starts at 10:00'. I was taken aback by the coincidence and serendipity. I ventured into the room, where the workshop was being held and sat down. When asked why I was there, I stood up, explained why I was there and I think that all were surprised, including Fr. Nicholas. I listened and participated in the work-shop, which was about the 'Gifts of the Spirit'. After the workshop had ended, Fr. Nicholas gave me time to talk to him about my rage. To cut a long story short, I had to forgive my brother-in-law for his treachery, in order to release this anger. Fr. Nicholas and I prayed a special prayer asking Jesus to take this away from me and to heal me. I returned home that evening, in much lighter spirits.

In the following months, on different Saturdays, I attended *Healing Workshop I - Love and Forgiveness* and *Healing Workshop II - The Ministry of Deliverance*, which were educational and uplifting. I also travelled once again to Douai for a one-to-one meeting with Fr. Nicholas. He helped me to trace back my early memories. The memory of me as a child came back. I remember feeling abandoned at the age of 6 at boarding school in Fribourg, Switzerland, where my parents had left me to go on a tour of Europe by car. Fear and anger came to mind, not love. He told me that my anger with my brother-in-law was 'the presenting problem,' and that 'the real problem' lay in this earlier part of my life. Fr. Nicholas showed me how to pray to forgive my parents for what they had done; clearly they had not meant to hurt me. I prayed to forgive them and to love them. He placed his hands on my head and we prayed together a special prayer for my parents, for my brother-in-law, and for myself. By the end of that prayer, it was as if a heavy weight was lifted from me. I felt that forgiveness, which can be so difficult to do, extinguish the anger, allowing me to love again. Christ's healing is available to everyone; they simply need to believe in him. It seems so difficult, yet with humility, it's so easy.

In gratitude to our Lord and to Fr. Nicholas, I have offered to edit, design, and produce his manuscript into a book, so others can benefit, as I did.

George
22 July 2015

---

A search on the Internet for the word 'forgiveness,' at the time of writing, shows in excess of 67 million hits, which is a significant number. However, type in the word 'revenge' and the number is in excess of 170 million hits. The world is full of people who nourish resentment, plan retaliations and exact revenge, expecting naturally that it will result in quenching their pain, which it does not; in fact, it only makes matters worse. Forgiveness is the only antidote and there is a growing realisation of this fact in the secular world today. The iconic Mayo Clinic's website covers forgiveness in its healthy lifestyle section and declares that *'forgiveness is a gift you give yourself.'*[13] There is even a 'science of forgiveness', which posits that *'when you don't forgive, you release all the chemicals of the stress response.'*[14]

The physical benefits of forgiveness are not illusionary, but real and genuine, as the following abstract explains:

An abstract from a research published in December 2014, at Erasmus University in Rotterdam, Holland shows that in the aftermath of conflict, forgiveness improves the wellbeing of victims and the victim–offender relationship. Building on the research on embodied perception and economy of action, we demonstrate that forgiveness also has implications for victims' perceptions and behaviour in the physical domain. Metaphorically, unforgiveness is a burden that can be lightened by forgiveness; we show that people induced to feel forgiveness perceive hills to be less steep (Study 1) and jump higher in an ostensible fitness test (Study 2) than people who are induced to feel unforgiveness.

These findings suggest that forgiveness may lighten the physical burden of unforgiveness, providing evidence that forgiveness can help victims overcome the negative effects of conflict.[15]

## PRACTICAL

When you feel a healing taking place - **This is the beginning of the healing, not the end** - so we have to continue forgiving and loving. It is a state, a way of life, we are to be people who are forgiving and loving. Sometimes people come back to me saying that they thought they had been healed but it has come back again. I ask them if they had continued to forgive and love. 'Oh no, I forgot!'

In my workshops, I give out other sheets of paper, for instance The *Barbara Schlemon Prayer for Healing* I mentioned earlier as well as *The Forgiveness Prayer,* which starts off by saying, use this prayer for nine days as a Novena. Well, I went on a Retreat given by the writer of this prayer and the retreat was for priests. He gave us a beautiful gold covered leaflet

with the same prayer slightly extended with the last
two pages numbered and lined 1 to 15 and 16 to 30.
He told us 'I normally give this prayer to people to
say for nine days, but for you priests it's for 30 days.
I want you to be priests who are always in a state of
forgiving.'

Does God say: 'I **have** forgiven you?' or rather 'I **am**
forgiving you.' I'm sure it is the latter. God is
always in a state of forgiving and loving.

I like asking the following - *Forgiving* is made up of
two words; 'for' and 'giving.' How do you spell the
first word? When everybody answers 'for' I say, I
think it should be 'fore.' The word **foregiving**
(which doesn't exist) means to me, *giving away*
something beforehand – something that we have
been hanging on to for a long time, such as
*resentment.* So get rid of it.

Luke 6: 27-38, but in particular 37-38, 'Judge not,
and you will not be judged; condemn not, and you
will not be condemned; forgive, and you will be
forgiven;'

Jesus leads by example:

*'Father, forgive them for they know not what they do.'*
*Luke 23:34*

## The best example of forgiving

***Christ Crucified with the Virgin, Saint John, and***
***Mary Magdalene by Sir Anthony van Dyck, (c.1629)***
*Courtesy: www.pinterest.com/pin/258253359857627222*

*NOTES TO HEALING WORKSHOP I*
*1. www.vatican.va/archive/ENG0015/P17._HTM*
*2. www.vatican.va/archive/ENG0015/P20._HTM*
*3. Raniero Cantalamessa 'The Holy Spirit in the Life of Jesus', Chapter 20, page 20, para 1*
*4. ditto, Chapter 2, pages 21-22, para 3*
*5. ditto, Chapter 2, page 22, para 1*
*6. ditto, Chapter 1, page 9, para 3*
*7. ditto, Chapter 1, page 10*
*8. (http//restlesspilgrim.com from a blog entitled V2 - we love you - by kind permission of David Bates)*
*9. by kind permission of the Good News Magazine from an article written by Barbara Schlemon published in the 1970s*
*10. Healing the Hidden Self by Barbara Schlemon Ryan (c. 1978) the above is a precis of each section, written by Fr Nicholas Broadbridge*
*11.www.holyspiritinteractive.net/columns/peterdesousa/betterorworse/37.asp*
*12.www.holyspiritinteractive.net/columns/peterdesousa/betterorworse/toerrishuman.asp*
*13. www.mayoclinic.org/healthy-lifestyle/stress-management/expert-blog/forgiveness/bgp-20055972*
*14. salon.com/2015/08/04/the_science_of_forgiveness_when_you_dont forgive_you_release_all_the_chemicals_of_the_stress_response*
*15. 'The Unburdoning Effects of Forgiveness', byXue Zheng, Ryan Fehr et al, Feb. www.static1.squarespace.com/static/52b2693e4b0695bbec87ab3/t/549f860ae4b08d24cc61ffb6/1419740682117/Zheng+et+al+2014+SPPS.pdf*

# HEALING WORKSHOP

## II

# THE MINISTRY

# OF DELIVERANCE

Some twenty-five years ago, a lady came to see me with a problem, which I knew was beyond my capabilities because I suspected it needed a Prayer of Deliverance and at that time I had not been pushed by God into the Deliverance Ministry. I phoned an Anglican priest in London, Fr. Christopher Neil-Smith, who I knew could help, because he had written a book called *Exorcism* and had actually been seen on national television showing how he proceeded with a prayer of deliverance.

I took her to see him and he listened to her for some time and then said, 'Yes, there is something which needs our attention, so let's go into the church.' She knelt at the altar rails whilst he stood facing her and prayed. His hands were a good 12 inches above her head but they shook as he prayed. (I have seen this particular movement several times since then.) As he finished praying he said to me: 'Nicholas, a prayer for Light,' and I prayed with her for a moment asking Jesus and the Holy Spirit to fill her with light and peace.

We said our thanks and walked back to the Tube Station to return home. As we walked she said to me: 'Oh dear, as he was praying with me it was awful, dreadful, everything was black, but when you prayed it was marvellous, it was bright and heavenly.' Little did she realise that he had done all the work and that he knew how she might feel and that he had asked me to pray for light and peace, as I was the person, whom she knew.

It was some years later that I realised why he had asked me to say a prayer for Light when I read Matthew 12: 43-45 *'When the unclean spirit has gone out of a man...Then he goes and brings with him seven other spirits more evil than himself...'*

As we will see later, whenever we say a prayer of deliverance and the evil spirits go, we are left with a vacuum, which must be filled by the Holy Spirit.

I cannot now remember when I first started praying in the Deliverance Ministry. It was through praying with others in a group, who were praying for an individual, that I realised they were saying a deliverance prayer. Priests normally do not realise the power that they have through their ordination to help people to be set free. Remember in Healing Workshop 1, we talked about Jesus as the Messiah quoting from Isaiah 61 in the synagogue and the important phrase: *'to set free those who are oppressed.'*

## To set free those who are oppressed

A lady by the name of Ros Powell came to stay at Douai Abbey for a private retreat. She told me that she was a Catholic Christian evangelist, and she gave me details of her website. Later, I looked at her website and found that her mission statement is: *To increase Heaven and Decrease Hell.* On seeing it, I immediately realised that my mission statement is: *To Set Free Those Who are Oppressed*, which is also the subtitle of this book.

# THE MINISTRY OF DELIVERANCE[16]

## Introduction

*If you don't believe in the existence of personified evil, then reading the Gospels will make for uncomfortable reading. The Four Evangelists show Jesus face to face with the cosmic conflict between good and evil.*

## Jesus had a Deliverance Ministry

Luke 11:14, *'Now he was casting out a demon that was dumb; when the demon had gone out, the dumb man spoke, and the people marvelled.'* He was driving out demons and setting people free as he had promised, when he quoted from Isaiah in Luke 4: 18-21 *'...The Spirit of the Lord is upon me...to set free those who are oppressed.'*

There are many people, Christians among them, even Catholic priests, who deny the existence of the devil and demons, making out that they are a figment of our imagination. But in Ephesians 6:12 Paul says: *'For our struggle is not against flesh and blood, but against the rulers, against the authorities, against the powers of this dark world and against the spiritual forces of evil in the heavenly realms.'*

Remember from Healing Workshop I that Jesus used the Holy Spirit all the time: Luke 4: 18 – 21 *'The Spirit of the Lord is upon me. He has anointed me to preach good news to the poor...'* and as we progress from Healing to Deliverance he still uses the Holy Spirit as we shall see: Luke 11-14 *'But if it is by the Spirit of God that I cast out demons, then the kingdom of God has come upon you.'*

Since the Healing Ministry as a whole is an enormous subject, it is worthwhile saying here what are the main aspects. Deliverance is an extension of Healing and Exorcism is an extension of Deliverance. Therefore, and this is important, one does not go immediately to Exorcism, nor to Deliverance until the possibility of Inner Healing (see Healing Workshop1) is exhausted.

There are some churches and sects that see the devil everywhere and cause problems especially in families because someone tries to expel the devil from an unfortunate teenager and causes his or her death.

I wrote a letter to *Portsmouth People*, which was printed in June/July 2012, following an interview with the Portsmouth Diocesan Exorcist Oct/Nov 2011, saying that Deliverance should be more widely taught to everyone, as well as to priests. When exorcists write about exorcism they sometimes use the phrase *minor exorcisms*, which in fact means deliverance prayers.

As we have just noted, Deliverance should be seen as an extension of Prayer for Inner Healing. This implies that a prayer of Deliverance should not be said before a prayer for Inner Healing. If prayer or prayers for Inner Healing do not produce a result, then pray for Deliverance. Healing Workshop 1 was all about Inner Healing. I repeat, one does not go into the Healing Ministry and more so, one does not go into the Deliverance ministry. You are pushed into both by God.

Before explaining Deliverance I ought to make quite clear the use of the word *'evil'*. The problem as I see it is that as soon as you use this word *'evil'*, everyone immediately thinks of possession by the devil. It is not only the devil, but also a whole **range or gradation** of evil from the smallest vices or imperfections to the greatest of all which is possession by the devil. Possession by the devil is most uncommon, perhaps one in a hundred million people or less. At the other end of the range are small habits of sin or even something like smoking, can technically be called *'evil'*. If it is something I cannot give up, if I am bound by it, I am not free. I used to say I could give up smoking any time, but could I really? No, I was not free. So these are the two extremes of the word 'evil'. There is an apt analogy – for example, when we say someone is sick that could mean a sore throat or the last stages of cancer - the two extremes.

Christ came to set us free and that's what he wants to do if we are not free.

**The Devil and demons are mentioned time and time again in the New Testament.**

Here are a few scripture verses to look at:

Mark 1:13 *'He was in the wilderness forty days, tempted by **Satan**; and he was with the wild beasts...'*

Mark 4: 14-15 *'The sower sows the word. These are the ones along the path, where the word is sown; when they hear, **Satan** immediately comes and takes away the word which is sown in them.'*

Luke 4:13 *'When the **devil** had finished every test, he departed from him until an opportune time.'*

Luke 22:31 *'Simon, Simon, listen, **Satan** demanded to have you, that he might sift you like wheat...'*

John 13:2 *'...and during supper, when the **devil** had already put it into the heart of Judas Iscariot, Simon's son, to betray him...'*

John 13:27 *'Then after the morsel, **Satan** entered into him. Jesus said to him, 'What you are going to do, do quickly.'*

Ephes. 4: 26-27 *'Be angry but do not sin; do not let the sun go down on your anger, and give no opportunity to the **devil**.'*

Ephes. 6:11 *'Put on the whole armour of God, that you may be able to stand against the wiles of the **devil**.'*

1 Tim. 3: 6 *'A bishop… must not be a recent convert, or he may be puffed up with conceit and fall into the condemnation of the **devil**; moreover he must be well thought of by outsiders, or he may fall into reproach and the snare of the **devil**.'*

2 Tim. 2: 26, *'…and they may escape from the snare of the **devil**.'*

James 4: 7 *'Submit yourselves therefore to God. Resist the **devil** and he will flee from you.'*

1 Peter 5: 8 *'Be sober, be watchful. Your adversary the **devil** prowls around like a roaring lion, seeking some one to devour.'*

1 John 3: 8 *'The reason the Son of God appeared was to destroy the works of the **devil**.'*

## Jesus and his disciples often cast out demons

Matthew 8:16 *'That evening they brought to him many*

*who were possessed with **demons**; and he **cast out the spirits** with a word, and healed all who were sick.'*

Matthew 10:1 *'...and he called to him his twelve disciples and gave them authority over **unclean spirits, to cast them out, and to heal every disease and every infirmity.'***

Matthew10: 8 ***'Heal the sick**, raise the dead, cleanse lepers, **cast out demons**. You received without paying, give without pay.'*

Matthew 17:18 *'...and Jesus rebuked the demon, and the **demon came out of him,** and the boy was cured instantly.'*

Matthew 12:28 *'But **if it is by the Spirit of God that I cast out demons**, then the kingdom of God has come upon you.'*

Luke 11:20 *'But if it is by the finger of God that **I cast out demons,** then the kingdom of God has come upon you.'*

In the Sistine chapel in the Vatican, in the centre of

the ceiling, there is a painting by Michelangelo depicting the creation of Adam, showing God's finger touching Adam. The finger of God is the Holy Spirit. We know this because where Matthew (12:28) writes the *'...Spirit of God,'* Luke (11:20) writes *'...the finger of God.'* This is further confirmed because the finger of God in the third verse of the hymn: *'Come Holy Ghost, Creator come'* refers to the Holy Spirit.

Mark 3:14-15 *'...and he appointed twelve (Apostles), to be with him, and to be sent out to preach and have authority to cast out demons.'*

Mark 5:1-13 the demoniac in the country of the Gerasenes, the story ends: *'...the unclean spirits (Legion) came out, and entered the swine...and were drowned in the sea.'*

Mark 9:25 *'...and when Jesus saw that a crowd came running together, he rebuked the unclean spirit, saying to it, 'You dumb and deaf spirit, I command you, come out of him (a boy), and never enter him again.'*

***The Healing of the Gerasene Demoniac
by Andrew Madekin***
*Courtesy: http://andrey3377.livejournal.com/*

Then in v. 28-29, *his disciples asked him privately, 'Why could we not cast it out?' And he said to them, 'This kind cannot be driven out by anything but prayer.'*

Luke 9:1 *'...and he called the twelve together and gave them power and authority over all demons and to cure diseases.'*

Luke 10:17-20 *'The seventy returned with joy, saying, 'Lord, even the demons are subject to us in your name!' And he said to them, 'I saw Satan fall like lightning from heaven. Behold, I have given you authority to tread upon serpents and scorpions, and over all the power of the enemy; and nothing shall hurt you. Nevertheless* ***do not rejoice in this, that the spirits are subject to you; but rejoice that your names are written in heaven.'***

Acts 5:3 *'But Peter said, 'Ananias, why has Satan filled your heart to lie to the Holy Spirit and to keep back part of the proceeds of the land?'*

Acts 16:16-18 *'As we were going to the place of prayer, we were met by a slave girl who had a spirit of divination and brought her owners much gain by soothsaying. She followed Paul and us, crying out, 'These men are servants of the Most High God, who proclaim to you the way of salvation.'And this she did for many days. But Paul was annoyed, and turned and said to the spirit, 'I charge you in the name of Jesus Christ to come out of her.' And it came out that very hour.'*

Acts 19:11-12 *'...and God did extraordinary miracles by the hands of Paul, so that handkerchiefs or aprons were carried away from his body to the sick, and diseases left them and the evil spirits came out of them.'*

## Who is the Devil attacking?

The Devil attacks the Individual, the Family and small groups especially prayer groups of any kind, the Nations and the World, the Christian Community. *(At present he is also attacking married couples, and priests).* You see it happening all around us and on a large scale particularly wars between nations.

At the moment, in the Middle East, there is a war between Israel and Palestine, which has been going on since the time of Abraham's two sons Isaac and Ishmael. There is also another war between the Sunnis and the Shias in Syria, Iraq, and Yemen.

A web site called 'Wars in the World' lists, outlines, and describes each conflict in the world. In Africa, there are wars in 27 countries between 187 militant groups. In Asia, there are wars in 16 countries between 151 militant groups. In Europe there are wars in 9 countries between 75 militant groups. In the Middle East there are 8 countries at war between 218 militant. The most horrific example is the so-called Islamic State or ISIS, which is destroying everything in its path. In the Americas, there are 5 countries at war between 25 drug cartels and militant groups. In total there are over 65 countries at war with over 650 militant groups actively fighting.[17]

The devil is causing havoc all round the world, with extreme destruction and horrific violations against human beings, which is reflecting something in us, of the horrendous contents of the 'shadow' within our human nature. There is an innate capacity in every human heart to do terrible deeds of mercilessness. This is rooted in our fallen and sinful nature, but through baptism and with Jesus our Saviour we can overcome the world; we have been given the capacity to do good. Now is the time to invite for ourselves, and all humanity, the mercy of

God into our hearts, to transform this world, from its pain, lack of love, and division.

## The Individual

If someone is experiencing strong temptations or trials, say, anger, pride, lust, fear, discouragement, alcoholism, depression, especially when there is no apparent cause, there may be some degree of direct demonic attack.

When someone has a serious drug or other addiction problem, a really uncontrollable temper or is seriously involved in adulterous activity or pornography, worshipping money, gambling, always hypocritical, strongly tempted to suicide, or involved in the occult, there is more than likely some demonic bondage present.

The occult, like freemasonry, is like a hydra with many heads or like an octopus with tentacles, which doesn't want to be dislodged and needs special prayer. Through their own occult involvement, parents can even harm their children. Dr Kenneth

McAll, a missionary-surgeon, author of *Healing the Family Tree*, gives several examples of people affected by someone in their ancestry. His concern is mainly *the unloved dead* where no funeral or handing over of *the unloved* to God is done. He goes on to mention problem families where there has been an abortion and the dead baby has not been given a proper funeral and suggests a Eucharist being offered. (He was an Anglican). When this has been done, the problems disappeared.

Sometimes when I am praying with someone, the Holy Spirit prompts me to ask about any involvement in the occult or freemasonry. If they know for certain or think there may have been someone in the family involved, then I ask them to repeat after me: 'Lord Jesus Christ, I acknowledge you as my Lord and Saviour. In your Precious name Jesus, I abjure any connection with…and I ask you Lord to set me free from any after effects. Thank you Jesus.' *(The word 'abjure' means to swear against)*

This demonic bondage is often called demonic oppression, obsession or infestation. The devil has partial control and leaves other parts of the person free, so in many ways the person seems good **and is good**. It is important to remember this.

## Places

Sometimes places need a deliverance prayer of one kind or another. In Soho, London, a charismatic prayer group used to meet weekly. One day another of the sort of establishment usual in Soho was about to open. Their leader prayed to the Lord asking for protection and casting out the evil one - the next day it was gutted by fire. No one was injured. Several people from a similar group used to drive around the M25 asking the Lord to protect London.

## The 'Mystery' of the Bermuda Triangle[18] (*also the Devil's Triangle or the Devil's Sea*)

The story I always tell my group in a workshop is about the Bermuda Triangle. Dr. McAll and his wife were returning to England in 1972 on a banana boat, which was caught in a force 9 storm as the ship headed into the Sargasso Sea where a boiler burst and left them stranded. He and his wife heard a strange sound like a droning dirge continuously day and night. 'Could it be the Jamaican crew?' The captain said that was not possible. Then, Dr. McAll found a magazine containing diagrams of the old slave ships using the same route where two million slaves had been thrown overboard, with the merchants collecting more money for 'lost slaves' than by selling them in Virginia. Many other incidents have happened over the Bermuda triangle and one specific one that comes to mind is the five avengers, or 'The Lost Squadron', who were lost on December 5th, 1945.

When Dr. McAll and his wife arrived in England it occurred to them that they had heard the mournful dirge for a reason. Maybe they had a responsibility to pray for those wretched slaves who had died uncommitted to the Lord. In 1977, with some interested bishops and priests and some members of the Anglican Community of the Resurrection, a Jubilee Eucharist was offered on the same day throughout England. The curse of that dreadful place, where many ships and aircraft had been lost without trace seemed to have been lifted. Dr. McAll says that from the time of the Jubilee Eucharist until now, when he was writing in 1982, no known, inexplicable accidents have occurred in that area. I myself have searched several times on the Internet seeking information on the Bermuda Triangle and what he says is true. Maybe there is something after all in prayer!

Centuries-old traditions call for blessings on buildings and places to rid them of the influences of the dead. We used to bless houses in the old days! I myself was asked to bless the house my nephew and his wife had just moved into because they could hear strange noises. I blessed the house and the noises stopped. The ghost that is haunting a place may be a dead person needing prayer. If it is treated as such, Dr. McAll has never found the haunting to continue. I sometimes wonder if the spirit of the dead person is trying to attract attention in order to be set free.

**Ordinary measures to counteract the above or measures to avoid getting into such situations**

The above includes concentrating on Jesus and Holiness, Prayer and the Sacraments, a relationship with Jesus, Praise, Repentance, avoiding deliberate sin, the Our Father, Prayer to Our Lady, reading Scripture, establishing a relationship with the Good Angels and our Guardian Angel and with the Christian Community, Spiritual Counsellors, Holy Water, The Sign of the Cross, Crucifixes, Holy Pictures, Medals. Remember, it is Christ who saves, not these objects.

## THE ARMOUR OF GOD[19]

*The following may be helpful:*

Ephesians 6:11-17

1. I place upon my HEAD the HELMET OF SALVATION as a protection against all thinking, speaking, seeing, hearing, feeling which is not of you. (Christ)

2. I place upon my CHEST the BREASTPLATE OF

RIGHTEOUSNESS as a protection against all unrighteous thoughts, all fear and anxiety, all sickness and all harm to the body.

3. I place round my WAIST the GIRDLE OF TRUTH that I may be truthful at every level of my being.

4. I place on my FEET the SANDALS OF THE GOSPEL OF PEACE that I may be the messenger of your GOOD NEWS to others.

5. I take in my LEFT HAND the SHIELD OF FAITH with which to quench all the flaming darts of the enemy.

6. I take into my RIGHT HAND the SWORD OF THE SPIRIT with which to attack the strongholds of the enemy.

## REBUKING EVIL SPIRITS or praying a prayer of Deliverance[20]

Mark 6:7 and 12, and13. *'...and he called to him the twelve and began to send them out two by two, and gave them authority over the unclean spirits...So they went*

*out and preached that men should repent. And they cast
out many demons and anointed with oil many that were
sick and healed them.'*

Mark 16:17. *'...and these signs will accompany those
who believe; in my name they will cast out demons; they
will speak in new tongues...'*

According to the present discipline of the Catholic
Church, solemn exorcism of the possessed is
reserved to a priest (an Exorcist) appointed by the
bishop.   However, lesser forms of deliverance
prayer are permitted to Catholics, indeed we all
pray for deliverance when we conclude the Our
Father with the words: *deliver us from evil.*   The new
Catholic Catechism states (2851): *'In this petition, evil
is not an abstraction, but refers to a person, Satan, the
Evil One, the angel who opposes God.'*

### What can be done by any Christian?[21]

One can ask Jesus to deliver a person from a spirit
of anger, lust or fear for example.  Such a prayer is
not normally said out loud as it might frighten,

unless of course the individual is asking for such a prayer.

The following method is found to be helpful:

1. Start with praise and intermingle praise with the rest of the prayer. Praise is very powerful.

2. Prayer for protection of everyone present. Thus **'Jesus, put a ring of protection** around us with your Precious Blood, to keep us from harm. Holy Archangel Michael be our Defender, Mary, our Mother, be our Guide and our Protector.'

You may add: All the saints and the angels protect all present with their prayer. I set out here the prayer to Holy Archangel Michael:

St. Michael Archangel,
defend us in the day of battle.
Be our safeguard against the wickedness
and snares of the Devil.
May God rebuke him, we humbly pray,
and do thou, Prince of the heavenly hosts,
by the power of God,

thrust down to hell Satan,
and all wicked spirits,
who wander through the world
for the ruin of souls. Amen.

3. **Ask Jesus** to bind any evil spirits in the person who is being prayed for. For example: *'Jesus, please bind any evil spirits in John,'* or *'Jesus, please bind any evil spirit of anger or of fear in John.'*
(Exorcists have found that if they first 'bind' the spirits they are often easier to cast out afterwards.) It's also far safer for the one who is praying.

4. Then **ask Jesus** to cast out any evil spirits from the person in question. For example: *'Jesus, please cast out any evil spirits in John and command them not to return,'* or *'Jesus, please cast out any spirit of fear in John and command it not to return.'*

5. This is very important. Pray for the infilling of the Holy Spirit; for the departure of evil spirits can leave a vacuum, and one does not want them to return. (Luke 11: 24-26) *'Then he goes and brings seven other spirits more evil than himself, and they enter and*

*dwell there; and the last state of that man becomes worse than the first.'* For example: *'Jesus, please fill John's whole being with your Holy Spirit, so that there is room in John for nothing which is not of you.'*

I always add the **light** of the Holy Spirit. You may remember the earlier story of Fr. Christopher Neil-Smith and the lady I took to him and how he asked me to say a prayer for LIGHT.

The ordained priest prays slightly differently:

**After praise:**

As I am an ordained priest, I would recite:

1. *Lord Jesus Christ, put a ring of protection around us with your Precious Blood to keep us from harm. Holy Michael, Archangel, be our Defender, Mary, our Mother, be our Guide and our Protector.*

2. *In the Name of Our Lord Jesus Christ, with His power and with His authority, I bind any spirit from doing any harm to John, Mary or anyone connected with us.*

3. *In the Name of Our Lord Jesus Christ, with His power*

*and with His authority, I cast out any spirit of fear, etc.*
*4. Jesus, please fill John and Mary with your Holy Spirit.*
*Just let your Holy Spirit shine light and love in their*
*minds and hearts.*

## PRAYERS OF DELIVERANCE

In Healing Workshop I, I mentioned about Mike
Sarson and my talks to his people in Recovery from
Addiction and that day in November 2012, when he
talked about Meditation and I spoke on Recovery
from Addiction. I said in my talk that if I were to
pray a Prayer of Deliverance for them I would use
at least five named spirits: a spirit of rejection,
resentment, fear, anger and addiction. They said
'Yes'. I asked were there any more and they said
'Yes', and added: a spirit of shame, guilt, lack of self-
worth, to which I have since added, abandonment,
betrayal and recently I was given despondency.
There may well be also despair, hatred, obsession,
greed, pride, and jealousy. When I have mentioned
the first list of a dozen names to people with
problems but no connection with addiction, they
say 'these all apply to me'. From this I gather that

these named spirits will apply to most people with problems. I still pray Prayers of Deliverance with just one or two or three named spirits but I am always open to ask someone if any of the dozen named spirits resonate with them.

Unfortunately, bishops and priests do not realise that there are many ordinary people among us with relationship problems who suffer spiritually and who could be helped enormously with a listening ear and some prayer - *See the next story.* All we need is some training and a willingness to help. I'm told that parish priests have a lot to do and do not have the time, but I say they are spiritual fathers to their flock and the spiritual health of their flock comes first, not the administration of their parish, which so many priests have to deal with. I myself seem to have been very fortunate or blessed because in the five or six parishes where I was placed, most of the administration was done by a secretary or parishioners, so I know it can be done by delegating work.

\* \* \* \* \* \*

We mentioned in Healing Workshop I about Maria and her two daughters, Chantelle and Linda, but we delayed Maria's story until now as it concerned not only healing but also deliverance. She had told a friend she was going to phone the bishop and her friend said: 'Don't bother, he won't answer the phone.' She phoned and he answered. She mentioned briefly her divorce four years previously and that there was a lot of evil coming from her husband affecting both herself and the daughters. She did not want a do-gooder to pray over her, she needed an ordained man. She contacted me at Douai and I gave her an appointment and as I put the phone down I looked up and said 'Lord, what are you getting me into here? Maria tells us her story.

---

### Witness Statement Eight

### THE STORY OF THE MOTHER WHO PHONED THE BISHOP - Part 1 (2007)

I have been asked if I could say what difference

receiving deliverance from a Catholic Priest, Fr. Nicholas, has made to my life and the lives of my daughters.

I suffered from years of domestic violence: mental, emotional, psychological and sexual abuse. My ex-husband was too clever to risk getting involved with the police by committing acts of physical abuse.

Before receiving deliverance, the symptoms I was suffering were: mental chatter 24 hours a day and night, insomnia, panic attacks all day and every day, weight gain due to being tired all the time and just sitting exhausted, unable to work because I couldn't think. I would be in a constant state of freeze (beyond fight or flight) I would just freeze up and stare into space with PTSD. I would shake inside to the point that I would shake outside. The fear was off the scale, that I was too afraid to even cry, but if anyone (like a doctor) asked me what was wrong, I couldn't tell them for crying. I thought I had lost my mind, and that the damage to me mentally was irreversible. My hair was falling out and I couldn't take care of myself properly. The doctors I attended gave me anti-depressants and counselling. I even went to a Catholic Priest who put me in touch with the

Catholic Children's Society, where I saw a trained councillor who asked me what I wanted, and my reply was 'I have lost my identity, I don't know who I am any more.' I want some support so I can find myself, or more to the point, I felt as if I had lost my soul in the situation. The only thing I had not lost was my Faith in God, and that God was with me and would never leave me. I did not think this; I knew this to be true that no matter what was happening to my mind and body that God was with me. I felt like a Zombie that was trapped in a horror movie, I wanted to be free of that nightmare.

At the same time that all this was happening to me, similar things were happening to my daughters. Both my daughters suffered from PTSD with different symptoms; my youngest daughter gained lots of weight going up to a size 20 from a size 12 and about 6 or 7 stone. Both daughters became aggressive and bad tempered. It was as if the negative spirits attached to us fed off the fights and arguments in the house. I started to realise that being called to court by my ex-husband every couple of months was to continue the abuse. He would use the situation to lie about me and attack me verbally. The barristers never understood what was happening and said it was good for the Judge to see what he was like, they never realised what he was doing to set my recovery back. After one visit to the high court in London I was so stressed out that I reversed my car out of my drive into a parked vehicle, the reason was I was too spaced out to even see the other vehicle.

I have always been very sensitive to energies, what people call psychic, I would prefer to call it Mystic. The church doesn't talk about such things, even though the early church believed in Saints that received messages, healing the sick, casting out demons. So before I could go for help from the church I had to go to several doctors, councillors, I had acupuncture, and all these things were costly but did not clear or even help the problem.

Years ago I had asked for help from the clergy after our home had become disturbed with poltergeist and rats, mice, and flies in the loft. The house was less than 20 years old and the council (who dealt with the rat and mice said you never get both in the same place). I asked the Parish priest to say a Mass in the house and it cleared the energy; we had peace for just over a year, before it started again. The next time I contacted the Bishop of the area where I used to live and I was given permission to contact a priest to come and bless the house clearing the spirits. My ex-husband would not allow another Mass in the house (he had been away at the time of the first Mass). In the end I knew I needed to leave my husband to get away from these happenings and to find peace. I took many years to get the courage to leave my husband and apply for a divorce and an annulment. I suffered many years of strange happenings in my home, which I now know was connected to the lifestyle of my ex-husband (other women, lying, cheating, fraud, swearing, and sexual abuse). In fact the day I made the decision to divorce my husband it was because I received a message (the words just came into my head – 'if a hand causes you to sin cut it off') I knew it was talking about my husband. I had done my best trying to keep the family together, now I felt I had permission from above to seek a divorce.

I had to be very careful whom I told about the problems in the house, because it was the excuse my husband was looking for so the doctors could say I had mental problems and take the children into care. My ex-husband is very destructive to everyone he meets and even to his own children. He stood trial in

2006 for sexual abuse of our youngest daughter, the trial was stopped on the third day and he was allowed to go free due to the fact that our youngest daughter was too traumatised to give her evidence. She couldn't speak after being cross examined by the defence. She has now been healed with a Prayer of Deliverance. From 1968 to the present (all the time I have had dealings with my ex-husband) I have suffered from negative spirit activity. In the early years I was too afraid of being called crazy to ask for help, and the church was even less sympathetic than it is now. I was told to go to Mass more or pray more. I went to Mass daily, and all my life I have prayed daily.

One day out of desperation and many hours of prayer, I picked up the phone and called Bishop Crispin Hollis. I was lucky because he picked up the phone. I said I need your help, I don't know what to do or who to go to. I explained everything that had happened to me and my daughters and that I had seen all the doctors etc. I asked for the name of a priest who could help me (I also added please don't send me to a well meaning prayer group of do-gooders, I need an ordained man). The Bishop gave me three names but said: 'Ring Douai Abbey and ask for Fr.

Nicholas Broadbridge first, and tell him you were given his name by the Bishop.' So this is what I did, I was lucky again because someone at the Abbey answered the phone and passed my message to Fr. Nicholas.

My first visit with Fr. Nicholas resulted in me seeing the unpleasant spirit that was attached to me; it was between 3 ft. 6 inches and 4ft tall, like a sort of imp looking thing (very unpleasant) with a feeling full of mischief, like Gollum in The Lord of the Rings. My first night's sleep after the deliverance was a peaceful full night's sleep. At my first visit to Fr. Nicholas we talked mainly about Love and Forgiveness, after which he said a Prayer for Inner Healing, a Prayer of Deliverance and he anointed me. The mental chatter stopped, and it was heaven to be able to be at peace and in a quiet space in my head and mind. Other things followed like being able to think again and do things like writing letters and emails, also doing more than one thing at a time. In short I have been able to move on in my life, getting another job at the school, attending workshops (including Fr. Nicholas's Healing Workshop 1, 2 & 3). Most people don't know what it feels like not to be in control of your own life and thinking.

The severe depression lifted, and the fear left. Life became full of hope and happiness; everyday is an adventure and freedom again. Deliverance is the difference between being half dead and ill, and being alive and full of health and vitality. I have met people with similar problems who have turned to New Age, and pagan methods for help, therapists using crystals, pagan rituals etc. Just saying these things don't exist, doesn't make them go away. Saying a person has mental problems doesn't help anyone. Emotional problems are made worse by stress, and having these sorts of problems is very stressful. It all becomes a vicious circle, which the medical profession can't help, and even psychotherapists can't help by just talking about past traumas. In fact psychotherapy just increases the guilt because no matter how much the person tries to get well, it can't be done without help on the spiritual level.

I do seriously suggest that all priests should be taught to pray Prayers of Healing and Prayers of Deliverance. As I have just said, all these things cannot be helped simply by the medical profession or psychotherapy, there is always a need on the spiritual level.

Maria

---

## Witness Statement Nine

### THE STORY OF THE MOTHER WHO PHONED THE BISHOP - Part 2 (2011)

Since writing part one of these strange stories, life has got a lot better on a personal level, and I have now realised just how many people are in need of deliverance. I am able to see that many of the people who throw themselves under high speed trains are in need of deliverance, and not as it always says in the newspapers in need of a psychotherapist or psychiatrist. Many of the young people who commit suicide have university degrees and have lived normal lives in every other way, except they could not deal with the voices and chatter in their heads. I can remember one of the things that was said in the chatter in my head was 'it would be easy to end it all', to which I remember saying 'no it would not, because life does not end with death, it just changes, so that is not an option...I need a priest to help me out of this mental hell'. Looking back now, I can see that I was even aware of talking to someone/thing outside myself...sounds a good case for a psychiatrist!

Life doesn't become 'happy ever after' overnight, another thing I have realised is that the patterns that allowed the dark spirits to get a hold in the first place, have to be addressed. Things like Low Self Esteem, not loving the self and others enough, although I never suffered from addictions, these things I have realised have an effect in allowing dark spirits to get a hold of people (alcohol, drugs, debt, and many others, including the internet and games when allowed to take over one's life).

Forgiveness was probably the biggest issue, not only forgiving my ex-husband, but also forgiving myself for not loving myself enough and treating myself with the respect that I deserve. In my defence I have to say that when I went to school in the 50's it was still ok to beat children and scare them half to death with teachers and priests saying, 'I was a bad person, and because of my sins, Jesus was crucified.' I grew up with Catholic guilt, well known by all Catholics.

Healing is an on-going thing, and I feel that the Healing Ministry is not as strong in the Roman Catholic Church as it could be. It seems to be more active in many other Christian Churches. When I once pointed this out to a priest many years ago, his answer was that every Mass is a healing Mass. That may be true, but even though I attended daily Mass and said the Rosary on a daily basis, I still picked up dark spirits like a victim spirit.

I have attended Healing workshops given by Father Nicholas Broadbridge OSB at Douai Abbey, and have seen him on a one to one many times for healing of myself and my daughters.

The mental and emotional damage done to my daughters whilst growing up with an abusive and addictive Father, who was too arrogant to get help for himself, and blamed me and the girls for all the problems, was far more than I could have ever imagined. As we all became emotionally and mentally healthier, I realised that my oldest daughter could not relate to men, even in her 30's she was highly suspicious of them all. The result was panic attacks that needed healing from the fear. A Prayer of Deliverance changed that, but there is still a need for Deliverance. My youngest daughter was left with a problem with reality, instead of seeing what was really going on in life she would see what she wanted to see, or even see the world through rose-coloured glasses. Due to the fact that my youngest daughter is very sensitive, she put on a lot of weight due to being bullied and abused; her size was a UK size 20 instead of the UK size 10 that she is now since the deliverance. That is twice the size she is normally, an increase of 70 lbs due to emotional pain caused by the abuse.

Both daughters have highly successful careers, one being a solicitor and the other being an architect, and yet the need for healing carries on. Why does the world think that if you have a good education and career, you must be fine and without problems?
I am now 4 years down the road from the first deliverance after I phoned the Bishop, and I find re-reading Part I, I can hardly imagine that it was me, because with the healing comes a lightness and the fading of the memory. One doesn't forget how bad it was but it is as if it was in another life or another time...now I am free from trauma and fear.

I strongly feel that Pope John Paul II was correct when he said to Cardinal Ratzinger that every diocese should have an exorcist, and he should lead a team of priests trained in the healing ministry especially deliverance.

I have noticed that the fastest growing industry in this recession is the Holistic Healing Industry, and the reason for this is that people are not stupid and they know what is needed and what the National Health Service can't supply. It is a multi-billion pound industry and it includes complimentary therapies, such as working with Angels (a very Catholic area), psychic protection especially using Archangel St. Michael, Spirit Release using several different methods, Reflexology, Yoga, Tai Chi, Hypnotherapy, Naturopathy, Homeopathy, Acu-puncture, Herbal Medicine, several different forms of meditation and visualisation, and Reiki Healing are all main stream now, and can be supplied on the NHS for stress relief. In fact, I have been told today that a Church of England parish in Hampshire is now teaching healing with Angels, mainly because they feel the church needs to bring itself into the 21st Century and give people what they are seeking in the wider world of healing. The church may be safe being politically correct, but people will find what they need one way or another. It is my belief that the world is changing and people want their spiritual bodies taken care of. If the church is not there with a main stream healing ministry, then people will find what they need elsewhere. The church has a duty to protect people from getting involved with the wrong forms of spiritual workshops and training. It can only do this by taking an active part in the fight against the dark forces that are at work in the world. Deliverance should be as common as going to the dentist. You don't wait until your teeth are falling out to visit the dentist. I had to search to find a priest who knew anything about deliverance, and I needed the Bishop's recommendation to be able to speak to that priest, without him thinking I was crazy and in need of medical attention for a mental breakdown.

Maria

---

## Witness statement Ten

### THE STORY OF THE MOTHER WHO PHONED THE BISHOP - Part 3 (2015)

Life has moved on since 2007, when I first met Father Nicholas at Douai Abbey, but so has my knowledge and understanding about the power of love, forgiveness and healing (Workshop 1) and deliverance, (Workshop 2).

I now understand how healing works, by first removing the hurts and resentments. The forgiveness of Jesus heals past pains, allowing us to receive the gift of unconditional love from God, resulting in freedom to heal body, mind and spirit for others and ourselves.

Healing by proxy for people shows the power of prayer for others. (It helps in cases where people are so far removed from God that they can't ask for help). Great changes have happened in lives after this form of intercession. If there is a need for deliverance then that also can remove any negative spirits that are holding a person back from wholeness (and holiness).

I now work with people, usually non-believers or lapsed Christians as a Spiritual Advisor, specialising in Domestic Abuse Recovery (having trained with the Police and Women's Aid) also Trauma victims with PTSD. I also include the power of forgiveness for healing. I send to Father Nicholas many people who have a story of things that don't make sense and includes more than emotional or mental hurts. Many of those I send to Father Nicholas are unbelievers, but are desperate for help from their living hell. I tell them that Jesus heals and he does not care if you don't believe in him, because Jesus loves everyone, God's love is for everyone.

Over the past 8 years I have learnt a lot about clearing the way so the power of the Love of God can do the healing and change our lives. When St. Paul said the greatest of the gifts is love, he wasn't talking about the love humans have for each other, as that is a mere reflection of the Love God has for us (God's children). He was talking about The Love of God, or Agapé, a sacrificial love that is more powerful than we can understand.

I now teach The Power of Love to everyone through word and deed, sometimes I hit a wall of resistance from a person, but I leave them to Jesus. I pray for them and move on. I don't take it personally, I just hand it over.

Only on looking back can people see how far they have moved forward, and the changes in their lives (me included). My daughters have both moved on also, both live in the United States and my oldest daughter and her husband have a baby girl. Chantelle and Jon have separated (due to his PTSD from the war). Thankfully they have stayed in touch and are amicable to each other. Jon became a Catholic and carries his rosary beads around with him everywhere. Chantelle has just bought a house in the USA, and has her dogs. Life is a journey to be lived and thanking God for all we don't understand. Love is the answer to every problem, regardless of what it is. We live in a world where Money is seen as the most important thing, but as St Paul says without love nothing is of value. Money without love is greed; money with love is generosity.

I now attend every Healing Workshop at Douai Abbey with Father Nicholas. Many people have had miracles in their lives over the years. To quote a few: families have come back together, one lady found a family she didn't even know she had. Families that were heading for break-up are now happy and together as friends for the first time in years. Teenagers that were headed for failure in exams because of bad relationships with parents are now healed and at university, with a new value for themselves.

Spreading the love of God with all the gifts that go with it, is every Christian's duty. The gifts of The

Holy Spirit are for everyone; they are life-changing gifts (Workshop 3).

What I would like to see in the future is that more priests will be trained in the ministry of healing and deliverance, with an understanding of the power of forgiveness and love. Too much is talked about exorcism, which is very rarely needed, and not enough about deliverance as most problems are created by human sin (spiritual mistakes) and lack of forgiveness and love. As I said earlier, love is the answer to every problem, no matter what it might be.

Maria

---

## SAINT BENEDICT

The patron saint of our Benedictine community is St Benedict, who is also patron saint of Europe, and who struggled against evil and battled with the devil.

Saint Benedict of Nursia (c.480-c.547) left the decadence of Rome and eventually holed himself up in a cave to pray and do penance. He didn't run away from evil. He went 'into the desert' as a hermit to do battle with the devil.

## Jubilee Medal of St. Benedict

The origins of the Medal of St. Benedict are in doubt. During a trial for witchcraft at Natternberg near the Abbey of Metten in Bavaria in the year 1647, the accused women testified that they had no power over Metten, which was under the protection of the cross. Upon investigation, a number of painted crosses, surrounded by the letters, which are now found on Benedictine medals, were found on the walls of the abbey, but their meaning had been forgotten. Finally, in an old manuscript, written in 1415, was found a picture representing St. Benedict holding in one hand a staff, which ends in a cross, and a scroll in the other. On the staff and scroll were written in full the words of which the mysterious letters were the initials. Medals bearing the image of St. Benedict, a cross, and these letters began now to be struck in Germany, and soon spread over Europe. Pope Benedict XIV first approved them in his briefs of 23 December 1741 and 12 March 1742.

The Jubilee Medal below was first struck in 1880 to commemorate the 14th Centenary of St. Benedict's birth.

The blessing of St Benedict's medal is the only blessing of a medal, which contains an exorcism.

**The Benedictine Medal – Front**

In St. Benedict's left hand is his Rule for Monasteries. On a pedestal to the right of St. Benedict is the poisoned cup shattered when he made the sign of the cross over it. On a pedestal to the left is a raven about to carry away a loaf of poisoned bread that a jealous enemy had sent to St. Benedict.

Starting at St Benedict's right foot, going up and around are the words:

**Eius in obitu nostro praesentia muniamur**
*(May we be strengthened by his presence
in the hour of our death)*

Benedictine monks have always regarded St. Benedict as a special patron of a happy death. He himself died in the chapel at Monte Cassino while standing with his arms raised up to heaven, supported by the brothers of the monastery, shortly after he had received Holy Communion.

## The Benedictine Medal – Back

The four largest letters around the cross:
**C.S.P.B. - Crux Sancti Patris Benedicti**
*(The Cross of our holy father Benedict)*

Vertical letters inside the cross
**C.S.S.M.L - Crux sacra sit mihi lux!**
*(May the holy cross be my light!)*

Horizontal letters inside the cross
**N.D.S.M.D. - Non draco sit mihi dux!**
*(Let not the devil be my guide!)*

The outer letters stand for the words
of an elegiac couplet
*(starting top right)*

V.R.S. - Vade retro Satana;
*(Get behind me Satan;)*

N.S.M.V. - nunquam suade mihi vana
*(never suggest vain things to me)*

S.M.Q.L. - Sunt malaque libas;
*(What you offer is evil;)*

I.V.B.- ipse venena bibas
*(Drink your own poisons)*

In St. Mary's Church, Upper Woolhampton, next to Douai Abbey, there are six paintings on the life of St Benedict created by Gabriel Pippett (1880-1962), an artist, illustrator, and wood carver, including the one shown above. The story behind this particular painting is that St. Benedict lived for three years in an obscure cave, known to no one but the

*The devil throwing a Stone to Break the Little Bell of St Benedict's – Gabriel Pippett (1913)*

Courtesy: St Mary's Church, Upper Woolhampton, Berkshire

holy monk Romanus. Benedict's cave could not be reached except by a high and steep rock, which hung over it, and Romanus would send down food with a bell that would notify Benedict that he was there. One day in envy of their charity and reflection, the devil threw a rock and broke the bell.

Notwithstanding, Romanus did not fail to continue assisting Benedict.

A light-hearted look at the power of The Saint Benedict Medal:

For serious devil problems, please consult an expert. Try to find an old, holy, humble, penitential, well-educated priest. When you have found him, please call the Vatican. For low-grade demonic problems, here is a traditional manner of telling the devil to go to hell…the medal.

There is no use trying to cast out evil spirits from someone who does not want to repent e.g. from the occult, although I myself would pray quietly to God that they might repent.

**Warning:**

Dom Benedict Heron gives a warning to children in schools who are playing with ouija boards and tarot cards and also to some Halloween parties that go too far and fortune telling stalls in parish fetes.

**Footnote:**

Although the devil and his demons can give us a difficult time, as they did to Jesus during His temptation in the wilderness - if we are truly trying to follow Jesus and to trust in him, then we have nothing to fear from the power of darkness.

We read in the Letter of St. James 4:7 *'Submit yourselves therefore to God. Resist the devil and he will flee from you.'*

And in Ephesians 4:26 *'Be angry but do not sin; do not let the sun go down on your anger and give no opportunity to the devil.'*

And St. Paul writes in Romans 16:19 *'I would have you wise as to what is good and guileless as to what is evil, then the God of peace will soon crush Satan under your feet.'*

So in truth, Satan and the demons have more to fear from us than we have from them, if we keep our eyes fixed on Jesus and if his praises are on our lips and in our hearts. Alleluia!

*NOTES*

*16. the entire Healing II Workshop is adopted and adapted from 'I Saw Satan Fall, the ways of spiritual warfare' by Dom Benedict Heron OSB, published by New Life Publishing (2007)*

*17. 'Healing the Family Tree' by Dr Kenneth McAll, Sheldon Press, London (1986) chapter 6, page 59*

*18. www.warsintheworld.com/?page=static1258254223*

*19. 'I Saw Satan Fall, the ways of spiritual warfare' by Dom Benedict Heron OSB, published by New Life Publishing (2007) Chapter 5, pages 65-66*

*20. 'I Saw Satan Fall, the ways of spiritual warfare' by Dom Benedict Heron OSB, published by New Life Publishing (2007) Chapter 6, pages 69-70*

*21. ditto, Chapter 6, pages 70-71*

# HEALING WORKSHOP

# III

# THE GIFT AND THE
# GIFTS OF THE SPIRIT

## THE GIFT AND THE GIFTS OF THE SPIRIT

As we said in Healing I, the Holy Spirit's presence and activity in Jesus' life have not yet received the attention they once claimed in the early Church. For the past few centuries, the Church, and even some theologians today, have tended to look upon Jesus' baptism in the River Jordan as a minor episode in his life and therefore, we miss the realisation that this was in fact a **major incident in Jesus' life**.

At his baptism something happened that dramatically changed the course of his life.

Luke 3: 21-22 *Now when all the people were baptised, and when Jesus also had been baptised and was praying, the heaven was opened, and the Holy Spirit descended upon him in bodily form, as a dove, and a voice came from heaven, 'Thou art my beloved Son; with thee I am well pleased.'*

This dramatic change in his life was the gift of the Spirit's anointing.

*The Baptism of Christ
by Pietro Perugino, (1512)*

*www.wikiart.org/en/pietro-perugino/pala-
di-sant-agnostino-baptism-of-christ-1523*

The words *...and the Holy Spirit descended upon him in bodily form*; this gift of the Holy Spirit, told Jesus that he was empowered, and the words *...and a voice came from heaven, 'Thou art my beloved Son; with thee I am well pleased,'* are from Psalm 2, one of several in the Old Testament foretelling the coming Messiah, told Jesus that he was the Messiah.

## What is the gift of the Holy Spirit?

The gift of the Holy Spirit is to empower us to be witnesses to Jesus Christ.

Jesus, himself, told his disciples that they would receive this gift in
Acts, 1: 5 *'...for John baptised with water, but before many days you shall be baptised with the Holy Spirit.'*

It was given to the disciples and Mary (120 of them) at Pentecost.
Acts 2:4 *'...and they were all filled with the Holy Spirit and began to speak in different tongues, as the Spirit enabled them to proclaim...'*

Then Peter, who was preaching on Pentecost, said:
Acts 2:36, *'Therefore let the whole house of Israel know for certain that God has made him both Lord and Messiah (the Christ), this Jesus whom you crucified.'* Now when they heard this they were cut to the heart and said to Peter and the rest of the apostles. *'Brethren, what shall we do?'* And Peter said to them, *'Repent and be baptised every one of you in the name of Jesus Christ for the forgiveness of your sins; and you shall receive the gift of the Holy Spirit. For the promise is made to you and to your children and to all those that are far off, every one of whom the Lord our God calls to him.'*

Jesus said to the Samaritan woman:
John 4:10 *'If you knew the gift of God and who is saying to you, 'Give me a drink,' you would have asked him and he would have given you living water.'*

It is what John the Baptist meant in:
Matthew 3:11 *'I am baptising you with water, for repentance, but the one who is coming after me is mightier than I. I am not worthy to carry his sandals. He will baptise you with the Holy Spirit and fire.'*

Mark 1:8 *'I have baptised you with water; he will baptise you with the Holy Spirit.'*

Luke 3:16 *'I am baptising you with water, but one mightier than I is coming. I am not worthy to loosen the thongs of his sandals. He will baptise you with the Holy Spirit and fire.'*

John 1:33 *'I did not know him, but the one who sent me to baptise with water told me, 'On whomever you see the Spirit come down and remain, he is the one who will baptise with the Holy Spirit.'*

Jesus himself said to the disciples (120)
Acts 1:5 *'...for John baptised with water, but in a few days you will be baptised with the Holy Spirit.'*

Acts 1:8 '...but you will receive power when the Holy Spirit comes upon you, and you will be my witnesses in Jerusalem, throughout Judea and Samaria, and to the ends of the earth.'

Peter explains to his brethren about the power of the Holy Spirit:

Acts 11:15-16 *'As I began to speak, the Holy Spirit fell on them (gentiles) just as on us at the beginning. And I remembered the word of the Lord, how he said, 'John baptised with water, but you shall be baptised with the Holy Spirit'...'*

The gift of Baptism in the Spirit is often followed by the gift of tongues. The purpose of this gift of the Holy Spirit is primarily to **empower** us **to be witnesses** to Christ, and therefore essential to every Christian.

St. Paul asked some disciples in Ephesus:

Acts 19:2-7 *'Did you receive the Holy Spirit when you believed?' They answered, 'No, we have never even heard that there is a Holy Spirit.' And he said, 'Into what then were you baptised?' They said, 'Into John's baptism.' And Paul said, 'John baptised with the baptism of repentance, telling the people to believe in the one who was to come after him, that is, Jesus.' On hearing this, they were baptised in the name of the Lord Jesus. And when Paul had laid his hands upon them, the Holy Spirit came on them; and they spoke with tongues and prophesied. There were about twelve of them in all.'*

Authors Francis MacNutt and Rev. Tommy Tyson explain and expand on this subject:

## Being Baptised in the Holy Spirit by Francis MacNutt[22]

When we talk about praying for healing, we also need to go back and speak about the power that enables us to pray for healing. This is the power that came upon the early church on Pentecost. Those 120 in the upper room were already Christian and were indwelt by the Holy Spirit — Peter with the Apostles and Disciples — but Jesus had still told them to wait in Jerusalem until they were filled with power by the Holy Spirit. So it's important for us, too, to be filled with the Holy Spirit, as they were in the early church. If you are not sure that you have had your experience of Pentecost (it happened to me in 1967 in Maryville, Tennessee), I encourage you to read the Gospel of John 14–17 and the second chapter of Acts, and then read one of Dennis Bennett's books.

In the last *Healing Line*, I celebrated the life and death of our friend Tommy Tyson, so I thought you might like to hear how the Spirit came upon Tommy. At the time he was a young Methodist pastor and it was very early in the charismatic renewal in the early 1950's, when he didn't know any other pastors with whom he could talk. So here's the story about how Tommy took that then risky step (it's an excerpt from a talk he gave in 1968 to a group of Roman Catholic priests).

## How I Was Baptised in the Spirit
## Rev. Tommy Tyson

Every time I would question Rufus Moseley about this special presence of Jesus, he would talk about the baptism with the Holy Spirit as a means of coming into union with Jesus. God began creating a great hunger in my heart. I did not know, however, how to go about preparing myself for this baptism by the Holy Spirit. Nevertheless, the Lord slipped in on me. It happened in the men's Bible class at the church I pastored. The lesson that day was on Pentecost (in the Second Chapter of Acts). The teacher didn't know any more about it experientially than I did. When he finished with the lesson, he turned to me and said, 'Pastor, do you have something you'd like to add to this lesson?' I thought to myself, 'I have something I'd like to say, but I'd better not let them know it.' I wanted to get up and tell these men how desperately I'd been seeking for the experience that the lesson dealt with. But, when this idea came to my mind, I thought I'd best not speak it, because, if these men, who made up the official body of the church, discovered how inadequate I was, they would lose their respect for me. Then I would no longer have a ministry!

But then, this question came to my mind very forcibly: 'Do you want a ministry of your own making, or do you want to be filled with the Spirit of God?' Impulsively, I came up to the lectern and gripped it. It was the most difficult step I have ever had to take: I was willing to make a fool of myself in the eyes of those who had accepted me as their pastor. They loved me very much, and I loved them, so I felt I was sacrificing the most precious thing God had ever given me, and that was the pastorate of this church. In fact, it was so difficult that it has made every other step since then relatively easy.

Nevertheless, I told these men how empty I was, how much I really desired and needed what that lesson had dealt with. While I was making a real mess of the whole explanation, God came to my rescue. While I stood before these men, telling them about my need and desire to be filled with the Holy Spirit, God began to fill me. I didn't know what was happening. It was as if wave on wave of power that I had never thought possible began to wash through my heart and mind — my inner being. The first thing of which I became conscious was that I was no longer nearly so concerned about what these men might think about me as I was of a desire to bless them.

This breaking of my fear of public opinion was my first awareness of the baptism of the Holy Spirit. This whole experience came to a climax one evening in the parsonage as I was sharing what had happened to me with my friend Wayne McClain. As we shared together — again, without my knowing what really took place or how it happened — suddenly, from within, without any kind of outward manifestation, there came a revelation of the Lord Jesus Christ himself — from within me. And, in that moment, the Scripture came to my mind and flowed through my lips, 'God has made him to be unto me wisdom and righteousness and sanctification and redemption.'

I realised that life is a Person, and His Name is Jesus; that wisdom is a Person and His Name is Jesus; that sanctification is not just gritting your teeth and trying to do it, but it's a person, and His Name is Jesus. As I understand it, this is what is happening to me in my own life: Jesus being revealed from within.

---

## The Baptism With the Holy Spirit
## by Rev. Tommy Tyson[23]

What does it mean to be baptised with the Holy Spirit? The first disciples were commanded by Jesus to remain in Jerusalem until they received baptism with the Holy Spirit. Following the fulfilment of this promise on the day of Pentecost, the early Christian disciples offered this same privilege to all who would believe in Jesus. I would like to point out some of the basic features related to the common witness of Christians in describing the Spirit-filled relationship.

### Personal Union With Jesus Christ

The Holy Spirit, moving in sovereign power, brings a person into a fixed inward awareness of the resurrected power, presence and person of the Lord Jesus Christ. On and following the day of Pentecost, the first century disciples gave evidence of knowing the resurrected Lord in an intimate and vital union. They were conscious of His presence and power. They knew Jesus, the Resurrected Lord, in the power of holy affection. They experienced the fulfilment of His promise to them as recorded in John 14:19-20.

### Imbuement With Power

Jesus said, *'But you shall receive power, after that the Holy Ghost is come upon you'* (Acts 1:8). Dynamite has the power to blow up stumps. It does not have the power to rock babies to sleep. The power of the Holy Spirit is not vague and undisciplined energy. The Holy Spirit gives us the power - the ability - to fulfil the purpose for which we were made.

### Power to Be Ourselves

In the security of Holy Love, there is the power for the removal of masks and the revealing of the true self. The restoration to true selfhood is a gift of God through the power of the Holy Spirit. This is the meaning of Christian confession. Confession is agreeing with God concerning the revelation He makes of you. The same writer (St Paul) who said, *'I am the chief of sinners'* is also the one who said, *'I can do all things through Christ who strengthens me.'* This double confession is the evidence of the real work of the Holy Spirit. In the power of the Holy Spirit, we stop pretending about and promoting the self.

### Power to Worship

To witness the resurrection of the Lord Jesus Christ is to see all human history consummated in the light of redemptive purposes. It is to see our needs in the light of the provision of God's grace. This insight within the human heart brings power for real worship. The glory of the presence of the resurrected Lord enables the Christian to sing the wondrous song of the soul.

### Power to Witness

The words, *'Enter to Worship, Depart to Serve,'* have often appeared on church bulletins. The New Testament genus is that we enter to worship in order to keep on worshipping as we move the altar from the Upper Room to the marketplace. Our work becomes our worship, and our worship becomes our work. The baptism of the Holy Spirit enables the believer to stay aware of the presence of the Lord in such a way that all of life becomes an act of worship.

## Power to Be Like Jesus

One of the most valid witnesses to the resurrection of Jesus is that there is very little difference in the ministry of Jesus before the crucifixion and the lives of the disciples after the resurrection. You catch the same courage, the same love, and the same concern for human involvement. You see the same abandonment of self to the call of the Holy Spirit.

Jesus has said, *'He that believeth in me, the works that I do shall he do also; and greater works than these shall he do because I go unto my Father'* (*John 14:12*). The validity of Christian experience is made manifest in the ability to produce the works of the glorified Lord. The gifts and fruits of the Spirit in the life of the believer are to glorify Jesus Christ among His people. (For gifts, read 1Cor. 12: 8-11 and for fruits, read Gal. 5: 22-23)

## Power to Integrate Spirit and Body

Another factor related to the baptism with the Holy Spirit is the relationship of the baptised person to both the Christian and non-Christian worlds. There is evidence of dissension among the Twelve as they lived in union with Jesus before the crucifixion. There is further evidence of differences and problems in the life of the Early Church as they were filled with and led by the Holy Spirit.

Nowhere is the cross more evident as a way of life than in the Christian's ability to die to the body of Christ in order to reconcile the tension between individual and corporate experience. This is the challenge of the Spirit-filled walk. This reconciliation means neither a denial of personal convictions nor a cheap imitation of the experiences of other people. It means a realisation that people are more important than ideas. Differences are to be used as avenues of growth and not as opportunities to divide.

The baptised person accepts his oneness with the body of Christ. This oneness transcends geographical, cultural, racial and political boundaries. The baptism with the Holy Spirit is a relationship with Jesus Christ that causes a deep desire to see this same love made manifest throughout the total body of Christ.

The Spirit-filled Christian is baptised by one Spirit into the body of Christ. His or her life becomes a deposit of grace and makes that person know that his or her body is the temple of the living God. Every circumstance of the Spirit-filled Christian becomes an occasion to manifest the inward relationship with the life of Jesus in thought, word and deed. Even in the midst of apparent defeat, we know that we are destined to be a part of the answer to the prayer: *'Thy Kingdom come, Thy will be done on earth as it is in Heaven.'*

---

# THE GIFTS OF THE SPIRIT

There are two types of gifts:

1. Gifts for the personal sanctification of each individual:

Wisdom, Understanding, Counsel, Fortitude, Knowledge, Piety, and Fear of the Lord - not fright fear, but awe (Isaiah 11:2-3)

2. Gifts given for the common good, which are called extraordinary gifts of the Holy Spirit are given to anyone but always for the good of others, for building up community:

Wisdom, Knowledge, Faith, Healing, Miracles, Prophecy, Discernment, Tongues, and Interpretation of tongues (1Cor: 12: 8-11)

**Wisdom**

The gift of wisdom is the special ability that God the Father gives to know the mind of the Holy Spirit in such a way as to receive insight into how knowledge may best be applied to specific needs. This gift is the revelation of God's infinite wisdom. It will be the solution to the problem at hand.

Here are a few illustrations:

Perhaps one of the most well known stories of

Solomon is about the two women, who were fighting over a baby, each claiming that the baby was theirs. (1 Kings. 3:16-28)

Solomon says, *'Bring me a sword.'* So they brought a sword for the king. He then gave an order: *'Cut the living child in two and give half to one and half to the other.'* Then the woman whose child it was said, *'Oh, my lord, give her the living child, do not kill him.'* With those words Solomon knew that this woman was the child's mother.

When I am listening to someone with a problem, I pray and then decide to say or do something… but it's not me; it's the Holy Spirit working through me.

Before a workshop, retreat, sermon, one prays asking for wisdom and knowledge. It's a form of remote preparation, in order to let Christ enter our hearts so he can come out of our hearts when we give the retreat or sermon.

## Knowledge

There are different ways that God can speak to us.

A good example in the New Testament would be when Jesus spoke to the Samaritan woman and said, *'No, you've had five husbands, and the person you're living with now is not your husband.'* Word of Knowledge is a revelation of a portion of God's knowledge that would otherwise have been impossible for that person to know. It can come as a thought, a vision, a word, a sense, or by an emotion or a scripture verse or a picture.

Here are a number of illustrations:

An example is when Peter received knowledge about what Ananias and Sapphira had done. Acts 5:1-11 But a man named Ananias with his wife Sapphira sold a piece of property, and with his wife's knowledge he kept back some of the proceeds, and brought only a part and laid it at the apostles' feet...Peter said, *'Why has Satan filled your heart?...You have not lied to men but to God.'* When Ananias heard these words, he fell down and died.

Elisha knew that Gehazi had lied to Naaman. II Kings 5:20-27 - *'Did I not go with you in spirit when the man turned from his chariot to meet you? Was it a time to accept money and garments, olive orchards and vineyards, sheep and oxen, menservants and maidservants?'*

Jesus instructed his disciples:

Matt 10:19 *'When they hand you over, do not worry about how you are to speak or what you are to say. What you are to say will be given you at that hour.'*

Matt 12:24 *'When the Pharisees heard this, they said, 'This man drives out demons only by the power of Beelzebul, the prince of demons.' But he knew what they were thinking and he said to them:*

*'Every kingdom divided against itself is laid waste…and if Satan casts out Satan, he is divided against himself, how then will his kingdom stand?…But if it is by the Spirit of God I cast out demons, then the Kingdom of God has come to you.'*

John 1:48-50 When Jesus told Nathaniel that he already knew him, Nathaniel answered, *'Rabbi, you are the Son of God.' Jesus replied: 'Because I said to you I saw you under the fig tree, do you believe me? You shall see greater things than these.'*

Mark 2:5 When a paralytic was lowered from the roof to be brought to Jesus, He said, *'My son, your sins are forgiven,'* but some of the scribes said it was blasphemy… *'…and immediately Jesus,* **perceiving in his spirit that they thus questioned within themselves,** *said to them, 'Why do you question thus in your hearts?'*

**Prophecy**

To prophesy is to proclaim a message from God while under direct inspiration of the Holy Spirit. It can be either encouragement *(Do not be afraid - your God is coming)* or an admonition *(Rev. 3: I know your works, that you have the reputation of being alive, but you are dead.)*

A prophecy is a divinely inspired utterance that edifies, exhorts, and comforts. It can declare what will happen in the future or it can be a reproof.

For example the evangelist Philip's daughters prophesied.

Acts 21:9 *'On the morrow we departed and came to Caesarea; and we entered the house of Philip the evangelist, who was one of the seven, and stayed with him. And he had four unmarried daughters, who prophesied.'*

St Paul teaches on prophecies, for example
1 Cor 14:1-40 especially '...*He who prophecies speaks to men for their up-building, and encouragement and consolation... He who prophecies is greater than he who speaks in tongues...'*

Matthew spends the whole of chapter 24 on prophecies.
Jesus left the temple and was going away, when his disciples came to point out to him the buildings of the temple. But he answered them, *'You see all these, do you not? Truly I say to you there will not be left here one stone upon another, that will not be thrown down.'*

This prophecy came true in AD 70, when the future Emperor Titus destroyed not only the temple but also the city of Jerusalem.
Another of Jesus' predictions to Peter was about betrayal.

John 13:38 *'Will you lay down your life for me? Truly, truly, I say to you, the cock will not crow, till you have denied me three times.'*

## Healing

The gift of healing is using God's healing power to restore a person who is sick, injured, or suffering.

Jesus healed all who sought him to be healed of their diseases.

Luke 6:19 *'And all the crowd sought to touch him, for power came forth from him and healed them all.'*

For example Peter and the apostles saw many people healed.

Acts 5:15-16 *'Now many signs and wonders were done among the people by the hands of the apostles... And more than ever believers were added to the Lord, multitudes both of men and women, so that they even carried out the sick into the streets, and laid them on beds and pallets, that as Peter came by at least his shadow might fall on some of them. The people also gathered from the towns around Jerusalem, bringing the sick and those afflicted with unclean spirits, and they were all healed.'*

## Miracles

Miracles are defined as Divine intervention to accomplish something that could not have been accomplished by natural means.

Let's look at the miracle of Jairus' daughter.

Mark 5:41 '...*Taking her by the hand he (Jesus) said to her, 'Tal'itha cu'mi'; which means, 'Little girl, I say to you, arise.' And immediately the little girl got up and walked.'*

Some people think this could be a healing. So when one compares this gift with the previous one above, there is a difference. Healing is God speeding up the process that could occur naturally. Miracles are God intervening and doing something that could not occur naturally.

### *The Raising of Jairus' Daughter*
### *by George Percy Jacomb-Hood (1895)*

*Courtesy: https://commons.wikimedia.org/wiki/*
*File:George_Percy_Jacomb-Hood_*
*The_Raising_of_Jairus'_Daughter_(1895).jpg*

For example another miracle would be the feeding of the 5,000 with five loaves and two fish:

Matt 14:17-21 *'...And they all ate and were satisfied. And they took up twelve baskets full of broken pieces left over.'*

## Faith

The gift of faith is not to be confused with the virtue of faith. The virtue of faith is one of the three theological virtues: Faith, Hope and Love. The gift of Faith is different as we see in 1 Cor. 12, which is one of the nine extraordinary gifts of the Holy Spirit, as mentioned at the beginning of this workshop.

This extraordinary gift of faith enables the person to have perfect confidence that God will bring about the desired effect. There is no room for doubt.

For example, when John reached the tomb, where Jesus had been buried, he went in and he saw and believed.

John 20: 2-9 *'Now on the first day of the week, Mary Magdalene came to the tomb early...So she ran, and went to Simon Peter and the other disciple, the one whom Jesus loved, and said to them, 'They have taken the Lord out of the tomb, and we do not know where they have laid him.' Peter then came out with the other disciple, and they went towards the tomb. They both ran, but the other disciple outran Peter and reached the tomb first; and stooping to look in, he saw the linen cloths lying there, but he did not go in. Then Simon Peter came, following him, and went into the tomb; he saw the linen cloths lying, and the napkin, which had been on his head, not lying with the linen cloths but rolled up in a place by itself. Then the other disciple (John), who reached the tomb first, also went in, and he saw and believed; for as yet they did not know the scripture, that he must rise from the dead.'*

On a light-hearted note, there is a story about this incident at the tomb, when John arrives there first and enters it. I was told this story that when a Jewish gentleman, of around Jesus' time, was at dinner attended by servants, at the end of the meal he would throw down his unfolded napkin as a signal that he had finished. However, if he folded his napkin, that signal meant: *I am coming back.* Now John saw *the napkin, which had been on his head, not lying with the linen cloths but rolled up in a place by itself* and interpreted it as Jesus saying: *I am coming back.*

Let's look at the gift of faith that Peter is given in healing the lame man.

**St Peter and St John Healing the Lame Man
by Nicolas Poussin (1655)**
Courtesy: The Metropolitan Museum of Art, New York

Acts 3: 3-8 '…*Seeing Peter and John about to go into the temple, he (the lame man) asked for alms. And Peter directed his gaze at him, with John, and said, 'look at us.' And he fixed his attention upon them, expecting to receive something from them. But Peter said, 'I have no silver and gold, but I give you what I have; in the name of Jesus Christ of Nazareth, walk.' And he took him by the right hand and raised him up; and immediately his feet and ankles were made strong. And leaping up he stood and walked and entered the temple with them, walking and leaping and praising God.'*

In the earlier miracle of Jairus' daughter, Jesus is asking Jairus to have the virtue of faith, while He himself had been given the gift of faith.

Mark 5: 35-36 *'While He was still speaking, there came from the ruler's house some who said, 'Your daughter is dead. Why trouble the Teacher any further?' But ignoring what they said, Jesus said to the ruler of the synagogue, 'Do not fear, only believe.'*

Joshua had absolute faith that the sun would stand still.
Joshua 10:12-14 *'Then spoke Joshua to the Lord in the day when the Lord gave the Amorites over to the men of Israel; and he said in the sight of Israel,*
*Sun, stand thou still at Gibeon, and thou Moon in the valley of Ai'jalon.*

*And the sun stood still, and the moon stayed, until the nation took vengeance on their enemies.'*

## Tongues

To speak in tongues is a divinely inspired utterance given in a language that has not been learnt by the speaker. When interpreted, this gift is similar to prophecy.

For example, at Pentecost, in the upper room:

Acts 2: 4 *'And they were all filled with the Holy Spirit and began to speak in other tongues, as the Spirit gave them utterance.'*

The disciples spoke messages in tongues to people at Pentecost:

Acts 2:7-12 *'And at this sound the multitude came together, and they were bewildered, because each one heard them speaking in his own language. And they were amazed and wondered, saying, 'Are not all these who are speaking Galileans?'*

St. Paul advises on tongues:

1 Cor. 14:27-28 *'If any speak in a tongue let there be only two or at the most three and each in turn; and let one interpret. But if there is no one to interpret, let each of them keep silence in church and speak to himself and God.'*

## Interpretation of tongues

Interpretation of a message in tongues by divine inspiration is given in the language of the speaker. It is not a translation but the speaker just gives the meaning. The purpose is to edify the church – and it is often a prophecy.

For example, St. Paul:

1 Cor. 14:5 *'Now I want you all to speak in tongues, but even more to prophecy...'*

## Discernment

This is to see beyond the outward appearance and have a revelation that distinguishes the nature of the spirit, which is at work. This gift discerns whether it is a human spirit, a demonic spirit, a godly spirit or the Holy Spirit.

For example, Peter discerned the spirit in Simon, who practised magic, wanting to have the power of the Holy Spirit for gain.

Acts 8:18-28 *'Your silver perish with you, because you thought you could obtain the gift of God with money...'* Another example is when Paul discerned the demonic spirit in the young lady, a fortune-teller:

Acts 16:16-18 *'As we were going to the place of prayer, we were met by a slave girl who had a spirit of divination and brought her owners much gain by soothsaying. She followed Paul and us crying, 'These men are servants of the Most High God, who proclaim to you the way of salvation.' And this she did for many days. But Paul was annoyed, and turned and said to the spirit, 'I charge you in the name of Jesus Christ to come out of her.' And it came out that very hour.'*

### Discerning spirits

(Greek: diakrisis) The spiritual ability to discern

from God's word between the spirit of evil and of God, the flesh and the spirit, and truth and error, before the fruit is evident.

St. Paul had this experience with Elymas the magician:

(Acts 13:8-11). *'But El'ymas the magician (for that is the meaning of his name) withstood them, seeking to turn away the proconsul from the faith. But Saul, who is also called Paul, filled with the Holy Spirit, looked intently at him and said, 'You son of the devil, you enemy of all righteousness, full of all deceit and villainy, will you not stop making crooked the straight paths of the Lord? And now, behold, the hand of the Lord is upon you, and you shall be blind and unable to see the sun for a time.' Immediately mist and darkness fell upon him and he went about seeking people to lead him by the hand.'*

Discerning spirits is about recognising what is of God as opposed to what is of the world, of the flesh and of the devil. Spirits can be summarised under three headings: the Holy Spirit, the diabolical spirit, and the human spirit. God's Spirit always inclines us to the good, working either directly or through secondary causes; the devil always inclines us to evil, working by his own power or through the allurement of the things of the world; the human spirit may be inclined to evil or to good, depending upon whether the individual follows the true path or selfish desires.

## JESUS USES THE GIFTS OF THE SPIRIT

### Wisdom

Matthew 4: 1 *'Then Jesus was led by the Spirit into the desert to be tempted by the devil.'*
Jesus answers three times from Scripture.

Matthew 5: 1-11 *'Blessed are the poor in spirit, for theirs is the kingdom of heaven...'*

Luke 6: 12-16 *'In those days he departed to the mountain to pray, and he spent the night in prayer to God. When day came, he called his disciples to himself, and from them he chose twelve, whom he also named apostles...'*

John 8:4 *'Teacher, this woman was caught in the very act of committing adultery. What do you say about her? ... Jesus bent down and wrote with his finger on the ground...he stood up and said to them, 'Let him who is without sin among you be the first to throw a stone at her.'*

Mark 7: 26 *'The woman was a Greek, a Syro-Phoenician by birth, and she begged him to drive the demon out of her daughter. He said to her, 'Let the children be fed first. For it is not right to take the food of the children and throw it to the dogs.' She replied and said to him, 'Lord, even the dogs under the table eat the children's scraps.'* This woman was given the gift of wisdom.

Mark 12:17 *'...Give to Caesar what belongs to Caesar and to God what belongs to God. They were utterly amazed at him.'*

Luke 7:6 *'...the Centurion sent friends to tell him, Lord, do not trouble yourself, for I am not worthy to have you enter under my roof. Even Jesus is shocked and says: I tell you not even in Israel have I found such faith.* The Centurion is given the gift of faith and wisdom.

Luke 1: 29-32 *Now there was a man in Jerusalem whose name was Simeon; this man was righteous and devout, looking forward to the consolation of Israel, and the Holy Spirit rested on him. It had been revealed to him by the Holy Spirit that he would not see death before he had seen the Lord's Messiah... Simeon took him in his arms and praised God, saying, 'Master, now you are dismissing your servant in peace, according to your word; for my eyes have seen your salvation, which you have prepared in the presence of all peoples, a light for revelation to the Gentiles and for glory to your people Israel.' And the child's father and mother were amazed at what was being said about him. Then Simeon blessed them and said to his mother Mary, 'This child is destined for the falling and the rising of many in Israel, and to be a sign that will be opposed so that the inner thoughts of many will be revealed—and a sword will pierce your own soul too.'*

Luke 2:36 *'And there was a prophetess, Anna, the daughter of Phanuel, of the tribe of Asher; she was of great age...she gave thanks to God and spoke about the child to all who were awaiting the redemption of Jerusalem.'*

Sometimes it is difficult to know if the gift belongs to one category or to another and often the gift can belong to one or more categories, such as wisdom or knowledge.

## Knowledge

Luke 9:18 *'Once when Jesus was praying in solitude, and the disciples were with him, he asked them, 'Who do the crowds say that I am?'...But who do you say that I am? Simon Peter said in reply, 'You are the Messiah, the Son of the living God.' Jesus said to him in reply, 'Blessed are you, Simon son of Jonah. For flesh and blood has not revealed this to you, but my heavenly Father.'*

John 1:35 *'The next day again John (the Baptist) was standing with two of his disciples; and he looked at Jesus as he walked and said, 'Behold, the Lamb of God!'*

Mark 2:5 *'Son, your sins are forgiven.' Now some of the scribes were sitting there, questioning in their hearts, 'Why does this man speak like that? He is blaspheming! Who can forgive sins but God alone?' And immediately Jesus, **perceiving in his spirit that they thus questioned within themselves, said...'***

John 1:48 Nathaniel to Jesus, *'How do you know me?'* Jesus replies, *'Before Philip called you, when you were under the fig tree, I saw you.'*

## Prophecy

Matthew 16:18   *'And I tell you, you are Peter and on this rock I will build my church, and the gates of the netherworld shall not prevail against it.'*

Matthew 16:21 *'From that time, Jesus began to show his disciples that he must go to Jerusalem and suffer many things from the elders and chief priests and scribes and be killed and on the third day be raised.'*

John 1:33 John Baptist - *'I did not know him, but the one who sent me to baptise with water told me, 'On whomever you see the Spirit come down and remain, he is the one who will baptise with the Holy Spirit.'*

Luke 1:46 And Mary said: *'My soul proclaims the greatness of the Lord; ...behold, from now on all ages will call me blessed.'*

Luke 1:67 Then, Zechariah his father, filled with the

Holy Spirit, prophesied, saying: *'Blessed be the Lord, ...and you, little child, will be called a prophet of God the Most High.'*

Luke 21:20 Jesus speaking to his disciples said, *'...When you see Jerusalem surrounded by armies, know that its desolation is at hand...'*

## Healing

Mark 1:31 *'Simon's mother-in-law lay sick with a fever. They immediately told him about her. He approached, grasped her hand, and helped her up. Then the fever left her and she waited on them.'*

Matthew 8:2 *'...a leper came to him and knelt before him saying, 'Lord, if you will, you can make me clean.' And He stretched out his hand and touched him saying, 'I will; be clean.'*

There are very many examples of Healing in the Gospels.

## Miracles

Mark 8:8 *'...And they ate and were satisfied; and*

*they picked up the fragments left over, seven baskets full. And there were about four thousand people.'*

Matthew 8:2 *'…a leper…saying, ' Lord, if you will, you can make me clean.' Jesus stretched out his hand and touched him saying, 'I will; be clean.'*

John 9:2-3 *'As he passed by, he saw a man blind from his birth. And his disciples asked him, 'Rabbi, who sinned, this man or his parents, that he was born blind?' Jesus answered, 'It was not that this man sinned, or his parents, but that the works of God might be made manifest in him.'*

## Faith

Mark 5:36    Jesus said to Jairus, the synagogue official, *'Do not be afraid; just have faith.'*
Jesus is asking Jairus to have the virtue of Faith while he himself has been given the *'extraordinary gift of Faith'* (1 Cor 12:9) given by the Holy Spirit.

John 9:2-3 *'And his disciples asked him, 'Rabbi, who sinned, this man or his parents, that he was born blind?' Jesus answered, 'It was not that this man sinned, or his parents, but that the works of God might be made manifest in him.'* Jesus has been given the *'extraordinary gift of Faith'* as later in the story he heals the blind man.

**Tongues**

We cannot say for certain that Jesus prayed in tongues, but these are my suggestions.

Luke 10: 21 At that very moment he rejoiced (in) the Holy Spirit and said, *'I give you praise, Father, Lord of heaven and earth...'* This rejoicing in the Holy Spirit is thought to mean praying in tongues because much of praying in tongues is praising God.

John 11:33 When Jesus saw her (Mary) weeping, and the Jews who came with her weeping, he was deeply moved in spirit and troubled...A Greek translation suggests something stronger – *to snort like a horse.* This suggests to me that Jesus was praying a prayer of deliverance in tongues against death, as sometimes happens when I am praying in tongues, which I know is a prayer of deliverance.

## Interpretation of Tongues

This would not apply to Jesus.

## Discernment

Matthew 16:21 When Jesus prophesied that he would suffer, be killed and rise on the third day. Peter says, *'God forbid, Lord! This shall never happen to you.'* Jesus replies, *'Get behind me, Satan! You are an obstacle to me. You are thinking not as God does, but as human beings do.'*

## One Story with several gifts

The story of Jairus coming to Jesus
Mark 5:22 *'My daughter is at the point of death. Please, come lay your hands on her that she may get well and live.'*
This is a gift of a miracle.

The above story is interrupted by the story of the woman afflicted with haemorrhages for twelve years, who had suffered much under many physicians and has spent all that she owned... She had heard about Jesus and came up behind him in the crowd and touched his garment... Jesus, **perceived** that power had gone out of him, immediately turned about in the crowd and said: Mark 5:30 *'Who has touched my clothes?'*

This is a gift of healing and knowledge (on the part of Jesus).

Mark 5:35 *'Your daughter has died; why trouble the teacher any longer?' ...'Do not be afraid; just have faith.'* Jesus is asking Jairus to have the virtue of faith, while he himself is given the 'extraordinary gift of Faith.'

Mark 5:41 *'He took the child by the hand and said to her, 'Talitha Cu'mi' which means, 'Little girl, I say to you, arise!'* Some people at first think that this can be both a miracle and a healing. No, she was dead, so it must be a miracle. The gifts in the above stories are knowledge, faith and a miracle.

I think that the best sentence in the bible is at the end of this story. He (Jesus) told them to give her something to eat – given that she's been dead for a day or two. It shows Jesus' compassion and humanity.

# QUIZ

*[Read the scripture verse and try to work out which is the gift for each]*

1. Matthew 16:23 Jesus to Peter: *'Get behind me, Satan! You are an obstacle to me. You are thinking not as God does, but as human beings do.'*

2. John 9 The man born blind. - Jesus said: *'Neither he nor his parents sinned; it is so that the works of God might be made visible through him.'*

3. Luke 1:36 Anna, the daughter of Phanuel, of the tribe of Asher... she gave thanks to God and spoke about the child to all who were awaiting the redemption of Jerusalem.

4. Mark 2:5 *'Son, your sins are forgiven.'* Now some of the scribes were sitting there, questioning in their hearts, *'Why does this man speak like that? He is blaspheming!* ...and immediately Jesus, perceiving in his spirit that they thus questioned within themselves, said...

5. Matthew 16:21 Jesus began to show his disciples that he must go to Jerusalem and suffer greatly.

6. Matthew 8:2 ...the leper: *'Lord, if you will, you can make me clean.'* Jesus stretched out his hand and touched him saying, *'I will; be clean.'*

7. Luke 1:46 And Mary said: *'My soul proclaims the greatness of the Lord; my spirit rejoices in God my saviour. For he has looked upon his handmaid's lowliness; behold, from now on all ages will call me blessed.'*

8. Matthew 5 *'Blessed are the poor in spirit, for theirs is the kingdom of heaven...'* (The Beatitudes)

9. Mark 8:8 They ate and were satisfied. They picked up the fragments left over, seven baskets full. There were about four thousand people.

10. Luke 9:18 Once when Jesus was praying in solitude, and the disciples were with him, he asked them, *'Who do the crowds say that I am?'* ...Simon Peter said in reply, *'You are the Messiah, the Son of the living God.'* [What gift is this?] Jesus said to him in reply, *'Blessed are you, Simon son of Jonah. For flesh and blood has not revealed this to you, but my heavenly Father.'* [What gift is this?]

11. Luke 7:6 The Centurion sent friends to tell him, *'Lord, do not trouble yourself, for I am not worthy to have you enter under my roof.'*

12. John 1:35 and as he watched Jesus walk by, John the Baptist said, *'Behold, the Lamb of God.'*

13. John 20:8 When Simon Peter arrived after him, he went into the tomb and saw the burial cloths there, and the cloth that had covered his head, not with the burial cloths but rolled up in a separate

place. Then the other disciple also went in, the one who had arrived at the tomb first, and he saw and believed.

14. Mark 1:31 Simon's mother-in-law lay sick with a fever. They immediately told him about her. He approached, grasped her hand, and helped her up. Then the fever left her...

15. John 1:48 Nathaniel to Jesus: *'How do you know me?'* Jesus replies: *'Before Philip called you, when you were under the fig tree, I saw you.'*

16. Matthew 4:1   Then Jesus was led by the Spirit into the desert to be tempted by the devil. Jesus answers three times from Scripture, for example, *'Man does not live by bread alone...'*

17. John 1:33 John the Baptist: *'I did not know him, but the one who sent me to baptise with water told me, 'On whomever you see the Spirit come down and remain, he is the one who will baptise with the Holy Spirit.'*

18. Mark 5: 25-30 There was a woman afflicted with a haemorrhage for twelve years. She said, *'If I but touch his clothes, I shall be cured.'* And after she touched him, Jesus asked, *'Who has touched my clothes?'*

19. Mark 5: 34 After the woman admitted what she had done, Jesus said, 'Daughter, your faith has saved you. Go in peace and be cured of your affliction.'

20. Mark 5:36 Disregarding the message that was reported, Jesus said to the synagogue official: *'Do not be afraid; just have faith.'* Which gift and who had the gift this time?

21. Mark 5:41 Jesus said *'Talitha Cu'mi,'* which means, *'Little girl, I say to you, arise!'* And immediately the girl got up and walked, (she was twelve years of age)

22. John 8:4 *'Teacher, this woman was caught in the very act of committing adultery.'* Jesus said *'Let the one among you who is without sin be the first to throw a stone at her.'*

23. Matthew 16:18 *'You are Peter and on this rock I will build my church and the gates of hell shall not prevail against it.'*

24. John 1:35 ...and as he watched Jesus walk by, John the Baptist said, *'Behold, the Lamb of God.'*

25. Acts 3: 6 Peter said, *'I have neither silver nor gold, but what I do have I give you: in the name of Jesus Christ of Nazareth, walk.'* There are two gifts - which ones?

26. John 13:38 Jesus answered, *'Will you lay down your life for me? Truly, truly, I say to you, the cock will not crow before you deny me three times.'*

27. Matthew 14:16-21 *'There is no need for them to go away; give them some food yourselves.'* Those who ate were about five thousand men, not counting women and children. There are two gifts – which ones?

28. Luke 6:12 In those days he departed to the mountain to pray, and he spent the night in prayer

to God. When day came, he called his disciples to himself, and from them he chose twelve, whom he also named apostles.

29. Luke 19:5 When he reached the place, Jesus looked up and said to him, *'Zacchaeus, come down quickly, for today I must stay at your house.'* What gift and how does he know his name?

## Answers to the Quiz questions

D = Discernment  F = Faith  M= Miracle
H = Healing  W = Wisdom  P = Prophecy
K = Knowledge

| | | | |
|---|---|---|---|
| *1.* D | *2.* F&M | *3.* W&P | *4.* K |
| 5. P | 6. H | 7. P | *8.* W |
| *9.* M | *10.* K | *11.* W&F | 12. K |
| 13. F | *14.* H | *15.* K | *16.* W |
| 17. K | *18.* K | *19.* H | 20. F |
| 21. M | 22. W | 23. P | 24. K |
| 25. F&H | *26.* P | 27. M&F | *28.* K&D |
| *29.* K | | | |

# Conclusion

I am now aged 86 and although I am still permitted to do one-to-one sessions, I no longer hold Healing Workshops at Douai Abbey, but I am hoping to continue.

Throughout my work in the Healing Ministry, my purpose in life, on reflection, seems to have been to help people to find out whom they have to forgive. I don't do the healing; I simply direct people to Jesus Christ, so that they can find healing from him. As St Paul says in 2 Corinthians 4:7 *'But we have this treasure in earthen vessels to show that the transcendent power belongs to God and not to us.'* I have simply been a catalyst.

Therefore, I have written this workshop manual as a testament of my life's work and I hope and pray that those who follow after me will benefit from this book.

NOTES TO WORKSHOP III
22. www.tentmaker.org/holy-spirit/baptised.htm
*by kind permission of www.christianhealingmin.org*
23. *christthehealer.us/article-gifts-of-the-Holy-Spirit-030318.html*

# APPENDIX

## RECOVERY from ADDICTION

In Healing Workshop I, I mentioned Mike Sarson, Founder of East West Organisation, a UK Charity, who has worked for 40 years with addicts, and addictions. I would like to add a little more about addiction and recovery. My talk at St Cassian's, Kintbury, started with the words: 'Has anyone, any government department, any NHS Trust, anybody at a meeting such as AA or NA, suggested to any of you that it may be helpful for you to find out why your addiction started?'

My opinion is that in every case of addiction there is lack of love. Not always from the parents, but the lack of love, from whatever cause, means that the addict is always looking for the love which they missed out on earlier in life. They continue looking for love in whatever form, be it alcohol, drugs, etc., without ever finding it. So I explain - you can pour water into my cupped hands and I can hold it, but try as I may I cannot grasp water. Love, like water, is to be received not taken. Letting the addict talk helps me to ascertain whom they have blamed and then I suggest forgiveness and love. It is not the forgiveness, which heals, but the love.

Mike Sarson adds that people all over the World are turning to substances to deal with their problems including alcohol, illicit drugs and prescribed medications. Mike also discovered that over 90% of people he assesses experienced a problem in childhood with a lack of love. This reinforces the need for a holistic approach to treatment, which embraces forgiveness and the healing of memories in order to make a full recovery.

# Acknowledgments

I was conducting a workshop one Saturday in the spring of 2013, when George Jerjian, an alumnus of Douai School came to visit me, hoping to have a talk. Having asked where he might find me, he was told that I was holding Healing Workshop 3. He came in, sat down, and stayed the rest of the day and a few months later completed workshops 1, and 2. Being an author of 9 books, he told me I had to write a book on my Healing Workshops. So my first thanks go to him, for not only badgering me into writing, but also for doing everything else leading to its publication.

Always in my gratitude are my fellow monks at Douai for nurturing me for over 60 years.

My special thanks also go to my family for supporting me and also to my niece, Marie-Colette Gradwell, for her efficient and professional editing.

Without Mary Flynn, not only would this book not
have existed, I would not have become a monk at
Douai Abbey.  Over 60 years ago, I was having
lunch in my firm's luncheon club, where she
worked and as I was leaving, she stopped me by the
door to say 'I saw you smoking your pipe just now,
have you ever thought of becoming a priest?' She
never ever mentioned it again.

I have to thank Fr. Clement Tiger S.J. for guiding me
through my year at Campion House, in Osterley; Fr.
Theodore Young O.S.B of Ampleforth Abbey for
sending me to Douai; Mary Tanner R.I.P. who sold
me Francis MacNutt's Healing, which started me off
on this journey; All the people in Charismatic
Renewal who taught me about Jesus; and especially,
Fr. Raniero Cantalamessa, whose book The Holy
Spirit in the life of Jesus, I have used constantly.

I am also grateful to my friend and prayer partner,
Zina Neagle, Oblate of Douai Abbey; Fr. Tom Taaffe
of Portsmouth Diocese who asked me to give the
three talks in the Alpha Course on the Holy Spirit,

which taught me a great deal; Barbara Bolton who supported me over many long years; Liz Martinez for helping me write my first draft; Carol Shepherd, who sends me people who need a prayer of deliverance and comes to every one of my workshops; Roddy Maddocks for his photographs of the wall panels of St. Benedict in St Mary's church, Woolhampton; and Mike Sarson, who not only comes to each workshop, but also knows the value of my workshops for his clients in addiction, and is working to produce a video of the first two workshops. Last but not least is my friend, Sue Furney, who has always helped me with printing the many papers we give in the workshops.

# ILLUSTRATIONS

The Healing of Ten Lepers
by James Tissot, (c.1890)
*Courtesy: The Brooklyn Museum, New York*

The Healing of the Blind Bartimaeus
by Harold Copping (1907)
*Courtesy: http://truthbook.com/newsletter/*
*the-healing-of-the-blind-bartimaeus-painting*

The Father Forgives the Prodigal Son
by Rembrandt van Rijn (c.1669)
*Courtesy: Hermitage Museum, St Petersburg, Russia.*

Christ Crucified with the Virgin,
Saint John, and Mary Magdalene
by Sir Anthony van Dyck, (c.1629)
*Courtesy: http://www.pinterest.com/pin/*
*258253359857627222/*

The Healing of the Gerasene Demoniac
by Andrew Madekin
*Courtesy: http://andrey3377.livejournal.com/*